MORE
MIDWEEK
MEALS

MORE MIDWEEK MEALS

NEVEN MAGUIRE

GILL BOOKS

Gill Books
Hume Avenue
Park West
Dublin 12
www.gillbooks.ie

Gill Books is an imprint of M.H. Gill and Co.

ISBN 9780717195527

Compiled by Orla Broderick
Designed by www.grahamthew.com
Photography by Joanne Murphy
www.joanne-murphy.com
Assisted by Dee Fahey
Prop styling by Charlotte O'Connell and Joanne Murphy
Assistants: Susan Willis, James Gavin, John Donnelly
Copy-edited by Kristin Jensen
Indexed by Cliff Murphy
Printed by Firmengruppe APPL, Germany

This book is typeset in DIN Regular.

The paper used in this book comes from the wood pulp of
managed forests. For every tree felled, at least one tree is
planted, thereby renewing natural resources.

For the management team at MacNean House
& Restaurant. Thank you for making our dreams
happen every day. Amelda and I appreciate your
loyalty and support very much.

ACKNOWLEDGEMENTS

I would like to thank all of the people who bought the first *Midweek Meals* book and gave us such great feedback. It was because of you that we decided to bring out this second volume. *Midweek Meals* encouraged people to cook at home and that is something I have supported throughout my career. So thank you all, and I hope you get a lot of new ideas from *More Midweek Meals*. Even Marty Whelan, my great Lyric FM friend, began cooking at home – no other book had achieved this feat! He has not poisoned the long-suffering Maria ... yet!

I have now been working with Simply Better at Dunnes for six years, and it has been a very interesting time. I enjoy meeting the many producers as the range is constantly expanding and I always get recipe ideas from working with these talented people. I was also thrilled to work with Dunnes on my cookware collection. Thank you to Margaret and Anne Heffernan for their constant support. Just watching their enthusiasm is always a tonic. Working with the Simply Better and cookware team on a daily basis is always a pleasure.

There is no better collaborator on a food book than the wonderful Orla Broderick. Thank you again, Orla, for your invaluable input.

And thank you to the team behind the book. Joanne Murphy photographed the food, and her attention to detail is second to none. She was ably assisted by Dee Fahey. Thank you to stylist Charlotte O'Connell and her assistants Susan Willis, James Gavin and John Donnelly. They did a great job. And thanks to Graham Thew for his beautiful design. Thank you to copyeditor Kristin Jensen and editorial manager, Aoibheann Molumby. As always, Nicki Howard saw the book through from beginning to end and was a joy to work with once again.

During all the disruption caused by Covid, I relearned the value of cooking and eating at home with Amelda, Connor and Lucia. These are precious years. There will be a lot more midweek meals in our house, and I hope readers get as much pleasure from these recipes as we do.

CONTENTS

ALL-TIME FAVOURITES

INTRODUCTION

I was bowled over by your response to *Midweek Meals* and, if I heard your feedback correctly, you want MORE!

It seems that, for many of us, the daily dinner dilemma can be a drag. Every busy parent can relate to that 5 p.m. sinking feeling when you get asked, 'What's for dinner?' But even if you're cooking for one, knowing during that hungry commute home that there's nothing inspiring in the fridge doesn't exactly lift your spirits.

I hope that this book will give you plenty more ideas in order to eat well every day. Now that many of us know *how* to cook, my focus here is on giving you even more inspiration for *what* to cook.

Try to get into the habit of dipping into this book every weekend and picking two or three meals for midweek. Before you know it, you will have significantly expanded your repertoire so that your evening meal will be something you look forward to.

ABOUT THE BOOK

This book is divided into four sections built around the way I like to cook:

1 ROASTING TIN

This section delivers stunning one-dish dinners. Just prep the ingredients, arrange them nicely in a roasting tin and let the oven do the work. I love that all these recipes give you the luxury of leaving food to cook itself without much attention. They're the perfect solution for anyone who doesn't like washing up or have the time or inclination to stand in the kitchen, stirring pots. The key message is that you can use any kind of tin, whether it's ceramic, enamel, Pyrex, stainless steel or even the bottom of a large casserole. As a rule, though, a standard 30cm x 37cm roasting tin is perfect.

2 MAKE AHEAD

I want to help you get organised! As our lives get busier, it can be hard to put a tasty meal on the table night after night. I hope that the recipes, tips and tricks in this section can help you reclaim your time with a little forward planning. Batch cook in advance at the weekends so that you have extra portions or make the freezer your friend for those busy nights when time is not on your side. Or if you're one of the many people who are now working from home, do some prep in the morning and get it into the oven in the afternoon. Be inspired with new ways to cook faster and smarter than ever before.

3 HOME COMFORTS

Brimming with new and interesting dishes to try from the wonderful world that is comfort food, my aim was to perfect the recipes so that when you taste them, they wrap their arms around you and give you a great big hug! It's really a collection of nostalgic and sentimental memories that will cheer anyone up. True comfort food doesn't just fill the stomach, it delights the senses too. For me, balance is everything.

4 ALL-TIME FAVOURITES

This section is packed full of tasty new twists on my personal favourites and the recipes I've got the most feedback from on social media. It celebrates all the things I love to eat and many of them are presented family-style so that everyone can just dig in and help themselves. I hope they bring some of the excitement of my travels and trying new dishes into your kitchen, showing just what you can do with standard supermarket ingredients.

THE SYMBOLS

You will see symbols at the top of each recipe that will give you useful information at a glance. You'll see how long each recipe takes to prepare and cook, whether it's suitable for a slow cooker (I use a Morphy Richards Sear and Stew 6.5-litre slow cooker), whether the dish freezes well (in which case, you could double up your efforts to have something for another day) and if the meal is packed with vegetable goodness.

 PREP TIME

 COOKING TIME

 LOTS OF VEGETABLES CRAMMED INTO THIS DISH

 SLOW COOKER FRIENDLY

 THIS MEAL FREEZES PERFECTLY

DEEP FREEZE

Think of your freezer as a back-up for the days when the fridge is empty and you don't want to make a trip to the shops. As a chef I appreciate the value of being able to get ahead and prepare things in advance, which is why I'm highlighting recipes that freeze particularly well. For those of us with busy lives, a well-stocked freezer is a welcome friend on a hectic weeknight. Pulling out a delicious homemade dinner is much quicker than the time it would take to phone and get a delivery for a takeaway, not to mention that it's also far cheaper and more nutritious.

FREEZING TOP TIPS
Make the most of your freezer by freezing things properly, following my handy tips.

- Always leave food to cool completely before freezing.
- Make sure you wrap food properly or put it in sealed containers, otherwise it can get freezer burn. Food should be wrapped tightly in cling film or if you use freezer bags, squash out any excess air before sealing them and lie them flat so that they stack nicely. Choose suitable rigid plastic containers that fit the contents with only a little room for expansion.
- Think about portion sizes before freezing. There is little value in defrosting a casserole big enough to serve six if you are a family of three. I often freeze food in single portions so that I can defrost only as much as I need.
- Try to freeze food when it is at its prime. If you have leftovers, decide if you are going to use them within three days – otherwise it's best to freeze them straightaway.
- Do not refreeze food once it has been thawed unless it has subsequently been recooked.

- Make sure food is clearly labelled and dated. I use a Sharpie pen for ease. In an ideal world, you would try to keep a record of the contents of your freezer and use older stock first.
- In the case of a power cut, don't panic. Food in an upright freezer will remain frozen for about 30 hours or 48 hours for a chest freezer. In the meantime, don't be tempted to open the door!

THAWING FOOD

- Freezing food does not kill bacteria. Once food is thawed the bacteria will start multiplying again, so thawing it overnight in the fridge is ideal. Once food is thawed, cook or eat it within 24 hours.
- The microwave is a good way to thaw food on the low or defrost setting (if in doubt, consult the microwave manufacturer's manual). However, it's a good rule to only thaw food in this way if it's going to be cooked or eaten immediately.

COOKING AND REHEATING FOOD

- Cooked food should be cooled as quickly as possible when placing it in the fridge or freezer for longer storage. Small quantities cool quite quickly, but larger quantities are best divided into smaller portions or transferred to a container with a large surface area. Do not cover food while it's cooling and ensure that it has been cooled and correctly stored within two hours.
- Leftover food can be stored in the fridge for up to three days in suitable containers.
- Never reheat food more than once. Make sure that it has been thoroughly reheated and is piping hot.

- If you have leftover rice, it's important to cool and chill it as quickly as possible. Spread it out in a thin layer on a tray, then as soon as it's cool, put it into a suitable container, cover and chill in the fridge. Keep rice for no more than a day before reheating it and then only reheat it once and ensure that it's piping hot.
- To avoid cross-contamination, never allow raw food to come into contact with cooked food. Put leftovers in a clean, covered dish to prevent cross-contamination. Store cooked foods on the top shelf of the fridge and raw foods on the bottom.
- Cooked meals can be stored for up to three months in the freezer, but the golden rule is: if in doubt, throw it out! For more detailed information, check out safefood.net.

CHAPTER 1 ROASTING TIN

15 MINS

 35 MINS

 LOADS OF VEG

Chicken, Halloumi and Chickpea Traybake Serves 4

1 x 400g tin of chickpeas, drained and rinsed

3 tbsp rapeseed oil

2 tsp dried harissa spice seasoning

4 skinless chicken fillets

250g baby plum tomatoes

200g Padrón peppers

125g halloumi cheese, cut into 1cm slices

sea salt and freshly ground black pepper

This traybake is best eaten immediately, while the halloumi is still hot, as it will go rubbery as it cools down. I just love the combination of the crisp, salty halloumi against the spiced chickpeas and lightly charred vegetables.

Preheat the oven to 180°C (350°F/gas mark 4).

Put the chickpeas in a bowl with half of the oil and the harissa. Season generously and toss until evenly combined.

Put the chicken, baby plum tomatoes, peppers and halloumi into a roasting tin and season with salt and pepper. Drizzle over the rest of the oil and mix with your hands to coat everything evenly. Add the flavoured chickpeas and roast for 20–25 minutes, until the chicken is tender and the vegetables are nicely charred. Serve immediately straight to the table.

15 MINS

 25 MINS

 FREEZER FRIENDLY (TRAYBAKE)

1 x 300g packet of mini chicken fillets, cut into thirds

1 large red onion, sliced

1 red pepper, sliced

1 yellow pepper, sliced

2 tbsp fajita or Cajun seasoning

2 tbsp rapeseed oil

2 x 250g pouches of cooked brown rice

1 x 400g tin of black beans, drained and rinsed

1 lime

100g thick Greek yoghurt

a handful of fresh coriander leaves, chopped, plus extra to garnish

sea salt and freshly ground black pepper

Chicken Fajita Traybake
Serves 4

Everyone loves chicken fajitas and this recipe is so quick to prepare. I've made it super simple by using pouches of pre-cooked brown rice, but if you have some rice left over, use that instead.

Preheat the oven to 220°C (425°F/gas mark 7).

Put the chicken, onion and peppers in a bowl with the fajita or Cajun seasoning and oil. Mix everything together using your hands, then spread it all out in a large roasting tin. Roast for 10 minutes, until the chicken is just tender and the peppers are starting to catch around the edges.

Remove the tray from the oven and tip in the rice and black beans. Give everything a good stir and return to the oven for 5 minutes to heat through the rice and black beans.

Meanwhile, cut half of the lime into wedges and set aside. Finely grate the rind and squeeze the juice of the other half into the yoghurt in a small serving bowl and stir in the coriander. Season to taste.

Drizzle over the coriander and lime yoghurt and scatter over some fresh coriander leaves before serving straight to the table with the lime wedges on the side for squeezing over.

15 MINS

 40 MINS

Sticky Teriyaki Chicken and Noodles Serves 4

2 garlic cloves, finely grated

25g fresh root ginger, peeled and finely gated

120ml soy sauce

2 tbsp light muscovado sugar

1 tsp chilli flakes

4 large boneless, skinless chicken thighs, trimmed

300ml hot chicken stock

225g dried flat rice noodles

200g baby pak choi, cut into quarters

2 tsp sesame oil

TO GARNISH

1 fresh red chilli, thinly sliced into rings

2 spring onions, thinly sliced

2 tsp toasted sesame seeds

A perfect weekday treat that delivers with fantastic flavours and very little washing up! Rice noodles are now in all the big supermarkets and the ones used here are what is traditionally used for pad Thai.

Preheat the oven to 200°C (400°F/gas mark 6).

Mix the garlic, ginger, soy, sugar and chilli flakes in a large bowl. Tip in the chicken thighs and smear until well coated. Arrange the chicken in a roasting tin, then pour the hot stock into the bowl with the remaining marinade and whisk to combine – you will use this later.

Roast the chicken for 25 minutes, adding a little water to the bottom of the tin if the teriyaki mixture starts to catch.

Put the noodles in a heatproof bowl and pour over enough boiling water to cover. Set aside to soak for 5 minutes, then drain.

Remove the chicken from the oven and transfer to a plate. Pour in the reserved teriyaki-flavoured stock, scraping the bottom of the tin with a wooden spoon to remove any sediment. Add the drained noodles and using a tongs, flip them over to coat them in the liquid.

Arrange the chicken thighs back on top. Nestle in the pak choi and drizzle lightly with the sesame oil. Return to the oven for another 5 minutes, until the noodles have absorbed all the liquid and the chicken is completely cooked through and tender.

To serve, cut the chicken into strips and divide between four serving bowls with the noodles, then scatter over the chilli, spring onions and sesame seeds.

15 MINS

 55 MINS

 FREEZER FRIENDLY

a knob of butter

400g boneless, skinless chicken (thigh or breast), cut into 2.5cm pieces

2 small leeks, trimmed and sliced

2 garlic cloves, crushed

finely grated rind of 1 lemon

1 tsp fresh thyme leaves, plus a little extra

2 tbsp rapeseed oil

175g sourdough bread

1 x 400g tin of cannellini beans, drained and rinsed

100ml hot chicken stock

100g crème fraîche

1 tbsp Dijon mustard

50g freshly grated Parmesan cheese

sea salt and freshly ground black pepper

TO SERVE

soft green leaf salad

Chicken and Leek Sourdough Gratin Serves 4

Use the leftovers of a sourdough loaf to make a delicious cheesy, golden topping. Serve with a salad or any green vegetable. The filling is lovely and creamy without having to go to the trouble of making a white sauce – perfect for a cold winter evening.

Preheat the oven to 200°C (400°F/gas mark 6).

Use the butter to grease the roasting tin and add the chicken, leeks, garlic, lemon rind and thyme. Drizzle over half of the oil and season generously, then toss with your hands until evenly combined. Roast for 30 minutes, until the leeks are softened and the chicken is just tender.

Meanwhile, tear the sourdough into small pieces and place in a bowl. Season and drizzle over the rest of the oil, tossing to coat.

Tip the cannellini beans into the roasting tin and pour in the hot stock, stirring gently with a spatula to combine, then fold in the crème fraîche and mustard. Scatter over the bread and sprinkle the Parmesan on top and another sprinkling of thyme. Bake for another 10–15 minutes, until crisp and golden brown.

Serve straight to the table with a separate bowl of salad.

25 MINS

 50 MINS

Roast Chicken and Potatoes with Aïoli Serves 4

4 chicken supremes (see the intro)

6 large shallots, peeled and halved or quartered

4 large potatoes, peeled and cut into chunks

2 tbsp rapeseed oil

1 tsp chopped fresh rosemary

½ tsp fresh thyme leaves

225g tenderstem broccoli

FOR THE AÏOLI

1 egg yolk

2 tsp lemon juice

1 tsp Dijon mustard

2 garlic cloves, crushed

100ml light olive oil (or use rapeseed)

75ml boiling water

1 tbsp chopped fresh tarragon (optional)

sea salt and freshly ground black pepper

This is a speedier version of a delicious roast chicken dinner but with a French twist. I've made a homemade aïoli that gets the juices from the pan stirred in at the last minute to take it to another level. Get the chicken supremes from your butcher – it's a skin-on breast on the bone with the first wing tip still attached.

Preheat the oven to 200°C (400°F/gas mark 6).

Place the chicken supremes in a roasting tin, skin side up, with the shallots and potatoes. Drizzle over the oil and season generously, then scatter the herbs on top and use your hands to mix, ensuring everything is evenly coated. Roast for 20 minutes. Remove from the oven and use a tongs to add the broccoli, turning it with the potatoes and shallots in the pan juices. Roast for another 15 minutes, until the chicken is cooked through and tender and the vegetables have crisped up nicely.

Meanwhile, make the aïoli. Place the egg yolk in a bowl with the lemon juice, mustard, garlic and a pinch of salt. Put the oil in a jug and slowly pour it into the egg yolk mixture in a thin stream, whisking constantly. This can be done by hand or with a hand-held electric mixer or food processor. Continue to add the oil, whisking continuously until the mixture has thickened. Season to taste. This can be made in advance and stored in a jar in the fridge for up to three days.

Once the chicken is cooked, transfer the chicken, shallots, potatoes and broccoli to a serving platter and cover with foil. Set aside in a warm place.

Put the roasting tin directly on the hob over a medium heat and whisk in the boiling water, scraping the bottom of the tin with a wooden spoon to remove any sediment. Bring to a simmer, then gradually whisk this into the aïoli and stir in the tarragon (if using). Pour into a small pouring saucepan and serve alongside the chicken platter, allowing everyone to help themselves.

20 MINS

1 HR 10 MINS

Chipotle Chicken Wings with Sweet Potato Wedges Serves 4

juice of 1 lime

2 tbsp rapeseed oil

2 tbsp honey

4 tsp chipotle paste

2 garlic cloves, crushed

1.2kg chicken wings, halved at the joint and trimmed

900g sweet potatoes, cut into wedges

FOR THE SAUCE

4 tbsp mayonnaise

4 tbsp buttermilk

1 tbsp apple cider vinegar

2 tsp horseradish sauce

1 tsp English mustard

1 garlic clove, crushed

1 tbsp chopped fresh dill

sea salt and freshly ground black pepper

TO SERVE

finger bowls of water with slices of lemon

I've cut chicken wings at the joint to make wingettes and drumettes so that they are easier to eat. Sometimes you'll find them like this in the supermarket, otherwise it's a quick job at home. The creamy sharpness of the Alabama white sauce perfectly cuts through the rich smokiness of the winglets and wedges.

Preheat the oven to 180°C (350°F/gas mark 4).

Mix the lime juice, oil, honey, chipotle paste and garlic in a small bowl, then season generously. Put the chicken into a large roasting tin and use your hands to rub them all over with the chipotle mix. Roast for 30 minutes.

Increase the oven temperature to 200°C (400°F/gas mark 6). Remove the chicken and add the sweet potato wedges, tossing to coat, then pour off any excess oil or use some kitchen paper to remove it if you find that easier. Return to the oven and cook for another 30 minutes, tossing a few times to coat in the glaze.

Meanwhile, make the sauce. Whisk together the mayonnaise in a bowl with the buttermilk, vinegar, horseradish, mustard, garlic and dill. Season to taste and transfer to a serving bowl. Cover and chill until needed. This can be made up to three days in advance.

Remove the tin from the oven and make room for the sauce. Scatter over the lime wedges and serve straight to the table with finger bowls of water and plenty of napkins so that everyone can tuck in – watch it disappear!

20 MINS

 1 HR 5 MINS

Chicken Saltimbocca with New Potatoes and Asparagus
Serves 4

750g baby new potatoes

2 tbsp rapeseed oil

1 garlic clove, grated

150ml chicken stock

8 slices of prosciutto

8 boneless chicken thighs (skin on)

a few sprigs of fresh sage, leaves picked

300g asparagus

sea salt and freshly ground black pepper

Saltimbocca literally means 'to jump in the mouth'. It's a traditional Italian dish normally made with meat wrapped up in sage and prosciutto. This version is quick and easy to prepare and is packed with so much flavour, you can't go wrong.

Preheat the oven to 200°C (400°F/gas mark 6).

Cut the potatoes lengthways into slices 1cm thick and put into a large roasting tin. Add half of the oil and the garlic, then season generously and toss to coat. Spread out into an even layer, then pour over the stock.

Tear the prosciutto slices in half. Open up the chicken thighs and season, then put a sage leaf on top of each piece and wrap loosely with the prosciutto strips. Nestle the wrapped chicken parcels on top of the potatoes and roast for 45 minutes.

Trim the asparagus, toss it in the remaining oil and season, then place in little bundles around the chicken along with a few more sage leaves. Roast for another 10 minutes, until the asparagus is tender and the chicken parcels and potatoes are cooked through and crisp at the edges. Serve straight to the table.

15 MINS

 55 MINS

 FREEZER FRIENDLY

Jerk-Spiced Chicken with Beans and Rice Serves 4

8 chicken drumsticks (skin on)

2 tbsp rapeseed oil

1 tbsp jerk seasoning

25g butter

275g basmati rice, well rinsed

1 x 400ml tin of coconut milk

350ml hot chicken stock

1 bunch of spring onions, thinly sliced

1 x 400g tin of kidney beans, drained and rinsed

2 garlic cloves, finely chopped

1 tsp fresh thyme leaves

sea salt and freshly ground black pepper

This recipe is a great example of letting the oven do all the work. As the rice is cooked underneath the chicken in the tin, you end up with lovely toasted bits as well as fluffy grains. Jerk seasoning is available in all supermarkets under the Schwartz brand or you could make your own with equal quantities of garlic salt, ground allspice, chilli powder and dried thyme.

Preheat the oven to 200°C (400°F/gas mark 6).

Rub the chicken drumsticks with the oil and jerk seasoning. Use the butter to generously grease a roasting tin. Add the rice, then pour in the coconut milk and chicken stock. Scatter over half of the spring onions along with the kidney beans, garlic and thyme and stir gently to combine. Arrange the chicken drumsticks on top, then cover with foil and bake for 30 minutes.

Carefully remove the foil and roast for another 15 minutes, until the chicken drumsticks are cooked through and golden brown. Garnish with the rest of the spring onions and serve straight to the table.

20 MINS

 1 HR 30 MINS

 FREEZER FRIENDLY

2 tbsp rapeseed oil

1 onion, thinly sliced

1 garlic clove, thinly sliced

2 large vine tomatoes, grated (skins discarded)

1 red pepper, thinly sliced

225g Iberico pork steaks, cut into bite-sized pieces

100g fresh chorizo, casing discarded and chorizo roughly crumbled

1 tbsp tomato purée

250g paella rice

a good pinch of saffron, soaked in a little just-boiled water

1 tsp smoked paprika

½ tsp fresh thyme leaves

600ml hot chicken stock

1 x 290g jar of grilled artichokes in olive oil, drained and quartered

sea salt and freshly ground black pepper

TO GARNISH

1 tbsp chopped fresh flat-leaf parsley

lemon wedges

Iberico Pork and Chorizo Paella
Serves 4

Dunnes has a fantastic range of free-range Iberico pork that has the most wonderful flavour and is a very special meat indeed. Of course, you could also use regular Irish pork steak with excellent results. A fresh green salad would also make a great accompaniment.

Preheat the oven to 180°C (350°F/gas mark 4).

Put the oil in a flat-lidded shallow casserole (or a regular roasting tin will also work with a double layer of foil as the lid). Add the onion, garlic, grated tomatoes, red pepper, pork, chorizo and tomato purée. Stir with a spatula until evenly combined, then roast for 20 minutes, until sizzling.

Remove the casserole from the oven and stir in the rice, saffron, paprika and thyme. Pour in the hot stock and season generously, stirring to combine. Arrange the artichokes on top in an attractive pattern.

Reduce the oven temperature to 160°C (325°F/gas mark 3) and cover the casserole with a tight-fitting lid (or cover the tin with a double layer of foil). Bake for 1 hour more, until all the stock has been absorbed and the paella has started to catch a little around the edges.

Scatter over the parsley and garnish with the lemon wedges to serve straight to the table.

15 MINS

 1 HR 5 MINS

 LOADS OF VEG

 FREEZER FRIENDLY

6 large carrots, cut into batons

3 parsnips, cut into batons

1 small turnip, cut into similar-sized wedges

1 tsp chopped fresh rosemary

3 tbsp rapeseed oil

4 dry-cured bacon chops or medallion steaks (unsmoked)

3 tbsp apple syrup or honey

1 tbsp kecap manis or soy sauce

sea salt and freshly ground black pepper

TO GARNISH

chopped fresh flat-leaf parsley

Bacon Chops with Glazed Root Vegetables Serves 4

The natural sweetness of the root vegetables is enhanced by the apple syrup, though you could use honey instead if you prefer. I've served the veg here with bacon chops or use dry-cured Irish bacon medallion steaks if you can find them.

Preheat the oven to 180°C (350°F/gas mark 4).

Place the carrots, parsnips and turnip in a large roasting tin. Sprinkle over the rosemary and drizzle with 2 tablespoons of the oil, then season generously and use your hands to toss everything together until well coated. Roast for 20 minutes, until the veg are tender and just beginning to caramelise.

Meanwhile, brush the bacon chops all over with the remaining oil and season them with pepper. Mix the apple syrup or honey and the kecap manis or soy sauce in a small bowl.

Drizzle half of the apple syrup mixture over the root vegetables and toss until evenly coated, then put the bacon chops on top. Roast for another 20–25 minutes, until cooked through and tender, basting the chops after 10 minutes with the rest of the glaze.

Scatter over the parsley and serve straight to the table.

25 MINS

 45 MINS

LOADS OF VEG

FREEZER FRIENDLY

2 x 350g pork fillets, trimmed well

16 dry-cured rindless streaky bacon rashers

225g black pudding, casing removed and roughly crumbled

2 parsnips, peeled and cut into batons

1 fennel bulb (fronds reserved), trimmed and cut into wedges

4 small eating apples, cored and quartered

2 tbsp chopped fresh sage, plus a handful of small sprigs

2 tbsp red wine vinegar

2 tbsp rapeseed oil, plus extra for drizzling

1 tbsp honey

FOR THE GLAZE

4 tbsp Dijon mustard

2 tbsp honey

sea salt and freshly ground black pepper

Stuffed Pork Fillet Feast
Serves 6-8

This traybake is a marriage made in heaven and looks spectacular straight out of the oven. Of course, you could use regular-sized fennel and parsnips and just cut the fennel into thick wedges and the parsnip into batons. It's perfect for feeding a crowd or keep half for another day.

Preheat the oven to 200°C (400°F/gas mark 6).

Cut a slit about three-quarters of the way into the pork fillets, along their full length, then use a rolling pin to flatten them out enough to fill this pocket with the black pudding. Place two large pieces of cling film on your work surface and line up half of the streaky bacon side by side on each piece. Place a slit pork fillet on top and fill with the crumbled black pudding.

Close up each fillet bit by bit, stretching the bacon and using it to seal the pork over the stuffing. Try to get the join underneath each fillet to keep it closed. Do this all the way along until each pork fillet is wrapped up like a big parcel, then wrap tightly in the cling film. This can be made in advance or frozen.

Put the parsnips, fennel, apples, sage, vinegar, oil and honey in a large bowl. Season generously and mix gently until evenly coated. Tip into a large roasting tin lined with parchment paper, put the stuffed pork fillets on top and roast for 35 minutes, then remove from the oven and give everything a good toss.

Brush the stuffed pork fillets with the mustard and drizzle over the honey for the glaze. Scatter over the sage sprigs and drizzle them with a little extra oil. Roast for another 5 minutes, until the bacon is crisp and the pork fillets are cooked through and tender.

Carve the pork on a small chopping board and serve on plates with the vegetables and apples, spooning over any juices from the tin. Garnish with the fennel fronds.

15 MINS

 45 MINS

❄ FREEZER FRIENDLY (WITHOUT KALE)

Sausage and Sweet Potato Traybake with Crispy Kale
Serves 4

12 good-quality pork sausages (see the intro)

3 sweet potatoes, peeled and cut into thick wedges

2 red onions, cut into thick wedges

8 garlic cloves, peeled

1 tbsp Cajun seasoning

2 tbsp rapeseed oil

225g curly kale, stalks removed and leaves torn into small pieces

sea salt and freshly ground black pepper

A super-simple dinner that all the family will love. All supermarkets and most butchers have a good selection of premium thick, meaty pork sausages in lots of different flavours.

Preheat the oven to 200°C (400°F/gas mark 6).

Put the sausages, sweet potatoes, red onions, garlic and Cajun seasoning in a large roasting tin and season generously. Drizzle over half of the oil and use your hands to toss until everything is evenly coated.

Spread the ingredients out in an even layer, keeping the sausages on top. Bake for 30 minutes, then give everything a good toss.

Meanwhile, put the kale into a bowl and drizzle over the rest of the oil. Season with salt and pepper and massage the oil into the kale.

Scatter the kale over the sweet potatoes and bake for another 5 minutes, until the sausages and sweet potatoes are cooked through and the kale is nice and crispy. Serve straight to the table.

30 MINS

 1 HR

 FREEZER FRIENDLY

150g baby spinach leaves

125g mascarpone cheese

2 tbsp snipped fresh chives

a pinch of ground nutmeg (optional)

8 large eggs

200ml milk

2 tsp Dijon mustard

25g butter, at room temperature

1 x 350g packet of croissant dough (6 pack)

150g dry-cured bacon lardons (O'Neill's has a great product)

175g mature Cheddar cheese, diced

200g cherry tomatoes, halved

sea salt and freshly ground black pepper

TO SERVE

caramelised red onion chutney

Spinach and Bacon Croissant Bake Serves 4

You'll get no complaints for this moreish bake that would also make a lovely brunch dish at the weekend. It can be made up to 24 hours in advance with the egg mixture kept covered in a separate jug. Then all you need to do is leave it to soak while you heat up the oven.

Put the spinach in a colander in the sink and pour over a kettle of boiling water. Leave to cool a little, then squeeze the excess moisture out of the spinach. Put it in a bowl and beat in the mascarpone and chives. Season with salt and pepper and the nutmeg (if using).

Break the eggs into a bowl and pour in the milk, then add the mustard. Season generously and beat until evenly combined.

Butter a roasting tin or dish that is about 23cm x 30cm and a piece of foil large enough to cover the dish. Open the packet of croissants and tear each one into three pieces. Scatter half into the bottom of the dish, then add dollops of the mascarpone spinach. Scatter half of the bacon, cheese and cherry tomatoes on top. Tuck in the rest of the croissants and fill in the holes with the spinach, then scatter over the rest of the bacon, cheese and cherry tomatoes. Pour the egg mixture on top and leave to stand for 15 minutes.

Preheat the oven to 180°C (350°F/gas mark 4).

Cover the tin with the buttered foil and bake for 25 minutes, until just beginning to puff up. Remove the foil and bake for another 10 minutes, until crisp and golden but still with the slightest wobble in the middle. Leave for 5 minutes before serving straight to the table with a small dish of the chutney.

15 MINS

 30 MINS

 LOADS OF VEG

Lamb Meatballs with Roasted Cauliflower and Pomegranate
Serves 4

1 large cauliflower

1 large red onion, sliced

4 tbsp rapeseed oil

1 tsp ground cumin

12 ready-made lamb meatballs

100g pomegranate seeds

20g fresh flat-leaf parsley, leaves picked and roughly chopped

20g fresh mint, leaves picked and roughly chopped

juice of ½ lemon

50g toasted pistachios, roughly chopped

sea salt and freshly ground black pepper

TO SERVE

tzatziki

This warm salad using a combination of roasted and raw grated cauliflower is a revelation and by roasting the cauliflower leaves too, nothing is wasted. Lamb meatballs are now being sold in packets in some supermarkets, but you could quickly make your own with some lamb mince, salt and pepper.

Preheat the oven to 220°C (425°F/gas mark 7).

Coarsely grate one-third of the cauliflower into rice-sized pieces and set aside in a bowl.

Break up the rest of the cauliflower into small florets and put in a bowl with the cauliflower leaves and red onion. Drizzle over half of the oil and sprinkle over the cumin, then season generously. Spread out in a single layer in a large roasting tin lined with parchment paper and nestle in the lamb meatballs. Roast for 20 minutes, until the lamb meatballs are cooked through and the cauliflower and onion are lightly charred and tender.

Meanwhile, add the pomegranate seeds and herbs to the raw cauliflower along with the rest of the oil and the lemon juice. Season to taste.

When the meatballs and cauliflower are ready, quickly transfer the meatballs to a plate and fold the roasted cauliflower into the raw salad.

Tip the salad out onto a large serving platter and arrange the meatballs on top. Scatter over the pistachios and add dollops of the tzatziki to serve.

10 MINS

 20 MINS

Lamb Chops with Cannellini Beans Serves 4

1 x 290g jar of grilled mixed peppers in olive oil

4 tbsp sherry or red wine vinegar

2 tbsp honey

pared rind of 1 lemon

a small handful of tiny rosemary sprigs

8 lamb loin chops

2 x 400g tins of cannellini beans, drained and rinsed

200g feta, cut into large cubes

200g black Kalamata olives, pitted

½ tsp fresh thyme leaves

sea salt and freshly ground black pepper

TO GARNISH

a handful of fresh mint leaves

TO SERVE

baby spinach salad

This gets cooked under the grill so that the lamb chops char and all their juices soak into the cannellini beans. There's tang from the peppers, piquant olives and creaminess from the feta, all combined with a baby spinach salad – it's a match made in heaven!

Preheat the grill to high.

Drain the peppers of the olive oil and cut into thick strips, then put a tablespoon in a large bowl, reserving the rest. Put the vinegar, honey, lemon rind and rosemary in a large bowl and season with salt and pepper. Whisk to combine, then add the lamb chops, tossing them to coat.

Put the peppers, cannellini beans, feta, olives and thyme in a roasting tin and toss with a little more of the oil until evenly combined. Arrange the lamb chops on top and grill for 10–12 minutes, until the lamb is sizzling and cooked to your liking, turning once.

Garnish with fresh mint leaves and serve straight to the table with a bowl of the baby spinach salad.

20 MINS

 40 MINS

 FREEZER FRIENDLY

1 onion, finely chopped

1 celery stick, finely chopped

1 green pepper, diced

1 tbsp rapeseed oil

12 ready-made beef meatballs

1 x 400g tin of chopped tomatoes

2 tbsp dark muscovado sugar

2 tbsp apple cider vinegar

2 tsp Dijon mustard

1 tsp Worcestershire sauce

1 x 400g tin of kidney beans in chilli sauce

1–3 tsp hot chilli sauce, to taste

1 x 120g ball of buffalo mozzarella

25g jarred jalapeño pepper slices, drained, plus extra to serve

sea salt and freshly ground black pepper

TO SERVE

crusty bread or rolls

shredded crisp lettuce

thinly sliced red onion

Sloppy Joe Meatball Bake
Serves 4

This takes ready-made meatballs up a notch in this cheesy bake topped with melting mozzarella. It would also be so easy to double up the quantity if you found yourself with a crowd of hungry kids to feed.

Preheat the oven to 180°C (350°F/gas mark 4).

Put the onion, celery and green pepper in a shallow casserole (or a regular roasting tin will also work) and drizzle over the oil, then toss until evenly coated and spread out in an even layer. Arrange the meatballs on top and season with salt and pepper. Roast for 15 minutes.

Pour the chopped tomatoes into a large jug and add the sugar, vinegar, mustard and Worcestershire sauce. Mix until well combined, then stir in the kidney beans. Season with salt and pepper and add chilli sauce to taste.

Remove the casserole from the oven and give everything a good stir, then pour in the tomatoes and kidney beans, mixing well to combine. Tear over the mozzarella and return to the oven for another 15 minutes, until the meatballs are cooked through and the cheese is bubbling.

Scatter over the jalapeño peppers and serve straight to the table with the bread or rolls and bowls of the lettuce, red onion and jalapeño pepper slices.

15 MINS

 25 MINS

Piquant Hake with Couscous
Serves 4

4 x 150g skinless, boneless hake fillets

1 small red onion, finely chopped

250g baby plum tomatoes, quartered

50g green Queen olives, pitted and quartered

1–2 tbsp capers, drained and rinsed

1 tsp white wine vinegar

2 tbsp rapeseed oil, plus extra for greasing

200g couscous

400ml boiling water

50g wild rocket leaves

a handful of fresh basil leaves

sea salt and freshly ground black pepper

A light, tasty fish dish that is packed fill of punchy flavours. The couscous is the perfect accompaniment to soak up all the lovely juices. Ask your fishmonger for nice thick pieces of hake from the middle of the fillet.

Preheat the oven to 200°C (400°F/gas mark 6).

Place the hake fillets in an oiled shallow casserole (or a small roasting tin will also work). Scatter around the red onion, tomatoes, olives and capers, then sprinkle over the vinegar, drizzle half of the oil on top and season generously. Bake for 15 minutes, until the hake is just cooked through and tender.

Meanwhile, put the couscous in a heatproof bowl and season with a good pinch of salt. Stir in the rest of the oil and pour the boiling water on top. Cover with cling film and set aside for 10 minutes (or according to the packet instructions) to allow the grains to absorb all the water. Fluff up the grains with a fork and gently fold in the rocket.

To serve, tear the basil leaves over the baked hake and serve straight to the table with the couscous.

15 MINS

 40 MINS

Salmon with Crispy Potatoes, Samphire and Gremolata
Serves 4

675g baby new potatoes, unpeeled and sliced

2 tbsp rapeseed oil

4 x 150g boneless, skinless salmon fillets

2 cherry tomato vines, each one snipped in half

40g samphire (see the intro)

a knob of butter

juice of ½ lemon

sea salt and freshly ground black pepper

FOR THE GREMOLATA

a good handful of fresh flat-leaf parsley leaves, roughly chopped

1 garlic clove, finely grated

finely grated rind of ½ lemon

2 tbsp toasted pine nuts

Samphire is a green vegetable that grows here and is a little like seaweed. The supermarkets are now stocking it in their herb sections, but you'll also see it on most wet fish counters. Its crisp texture and salty taste work very well here in this traybake, but fine asparagus spears would also be a good substitute.

Preheat the oven to 180°C (350°F/gas mark 4).

Put the potato slices in a colander and rinse in the sink under cold running water. Dry well with kitchen paper. Tip the potatoes into a large roasting tin lined with parchment paper and drizzle with half of the oil, then season with salt. Mix with your hands until evenly coated, then roast for 15 minutes.

Meanwhile, to make the gremolata, simply mix together the parsley, garlic, lemon rind and pine nuts.

Remove the potatoes from the oven and give them a good toss, then make room for the salmon and add the cherry tomato vines. Season with salt and pepper and drizzle over the rest of the oil. Return to the oven for another 10–15 minutes, until the salmon is cooked through and tender and the cherry tomatoes have started to split.

Five minutes before the traybake is ready to come out of the oven, put the samphire into a heatproof bowl and pour over just enough boiled water to cover. Leave for 4 minutes, then drain and stir in the butter.

Squeeze the lemon juice over the salmon, then scatter the samphire and gremolata all over the roasting tin. Serve straight to the table.

20 MINS

 25 MINS

 LOADS OF VEG

Sticky Sea Bass with Chilli-Spiked Coconut Greens
Serves 4

400g tenderstem broccoli

2 small courgettes, thinly sliced

1 garlic clove, thinly sliced

1 fresh red chilli, cut into strips

1 tbsp rapeseed oil

2 tbsp soy sauce

1 tbsp honey

2 tsp sesame seeds, plus an extra pinch

1 tsp wasabi paste or Dijon mustard

4 x 125–150g sea bass fillets

a 2.5cm piece of fresh turmeric, peeled and grated

1 heaped tsp freshly grated root ginger

1 x 400ml tin of coconut milk

200g dried flat rice noodles

100g mangetout

150g edamame beans

sea salt and freshly ground black pepper

Feel free to use any green vegetables you have to hand for this dish, such as baby asparagus, quartered pak choi, sugar snap peas or fine green beans.

Preheat the oven to 220°C (425°F/gas mark 7).

Put the broccoli in a roasting tin with the courgettes and scatter over the garlic and half of the chilli. Season generously and drizzle over the oil. Toss until evenly coated and roast for 10 minutes.

Meanwhile, put the soy sauce in a shallow dish with the honey, sesame seeds and wasabi or mustard. Whisk to combine, then add the sea bass fillets, turning to coat. Stir the turmeric and ginger into the coconut milk and season to taste. Put the noodles into a heatproof bowl and pour over enough boiling water to cover, then set aside to soak for 5 minutes.

Remove the vegetables from the oven. Quickly pour over the turmeric-infused coconut milk, then scatter the mangetout and edamame beans on top. Add the sea bass, skin side up, and drizzle over any remaining soy mixture, then sprinkle another pinch of sesame seeds on the skins. Bake for another 5–6 minutes, until the sea bass is cooked through and flaking and the vegetables are piping hot.

Drain the rice noodles, then tip into one side of the tin and coat in some of the sauce. Scatter over the remaining red chilli to serve.

20 MINS

 50 MINS

 FREEZER FRIENDLY

750g potatoes, unpeeled

3 tbsp rapeseed oil

6 tbsp fresh white breadcrumbs

3 tbsp freshly grated Parmesan cheese

8 x 75g skinless, boneless white fish fillets, such as pollock, whiting or hake

225g frozen petit pois

a small handful of fresh mint leaves

a knob of butter

juice of ½ lemon

sea salt and freshly ground black pepper

TO SERVE

mayonnaise swirled with sweet chilli sauce

Posh Fish 'n' Chips with Mushy Peas Serves 4

Crispy fish, chunky chips and comforting mushy peas: homemade heaven! This recipe makes it so easy you'll wonder why you ever did it differently. I like the fresh ciabatta breadcrumbs for this dish as they're nice and rustic.

Preheat the oven to 200°C (400°F/gas mark 6).

Cut the potatoes into thick chips and place in a bowl. Add a good pinch of salt and 1 tablespoon of the oil. Mix until evenly combined and spread out in a roasting tin. Roast for 25 minutes.

Put the breadcrumbs in a bowl with the Parmesan and a good pinch of salt. Stir in the remaining oil. Put the fish fillets on a plate and season generously, then use the Parmesan crumbs as a topping.

Remove the chips from the oven and turn them over, then nestle in the Parmesan-crusted fish fillets and bake for another 10–12 minutes, until the fish is just cooked through and the crumb is golden brown.

Meanwhile, put the petit pois in a heatproof bowl and pour over enough boiling water to cover. Set aside for 5 minutes, then drain and return to the bowl. Add the mint, butter and lemon juice and season to taste. Using a hand-held blender, blitz briefly to a rough purée. Spoon into a serving bowl.

Serve the fish and chips straight to the table with the mushy peas and a separate bowl of mayonnaise.

20 MINS

 35 MINS

 LOADS OF VEG

 FREEZER FRIENDLY

3 tbsp rapeseed oil

4 tsp balsamic vinegar

4 tsp honey

½ tsp chilli flakes

2 garlic cloves, crushed

1 tsp fresh thyme leaves

1 small pumpkin, peeled, seeded
and diced (you'll need about 675g)

1 x 500g packet of gnocchi

3 small red onions, cut into wedges

225g shredded kale (any tough
stalks removed)

1 x 125g log of goats' cheese

sea salt and freshly ground black
pepper

Pumpkin and Gnocchi Bake with Goats' Cheese Serves 4

This is a great all-in-one recipe that uses lots of supermarket ready-prepared products, perfect to get on the table at the end of a busy day with very little effort. If you can't get pumpkin, use butternut squash or sweet potatoes, which can also be purchased already chopped, meaning one less job.

Preheat the oven to 220°C (425°F/gas mark 7).

Put the oil in a small bowl with the balsamic vinegar, honey, chilli, garlic and thyme. Season generously and whisk to combine. Tip the pumpkin, gnocchi and red onions into a large roasting tin and drizzle over most of the oil, reserving about a tablespoon. Toss until evenly combined, then spread out in an even layer in the tin. Roast for 20 minutes.

Toss the kale in the remaining oil and use your hands to massage it to wilt it down slightly. Remove the tin from the oven and give everything a good toss to ensure it's cooking evenly. Fold in the dressed kale, then roast for another 4–5 minutes, until the kale is starting to crisp up, the gnocchi are golden and the pumpkin is tender.

Crumble over the goats' cheese, season with pepper and serve straight to the table.

15 MINS

 45 MINS

 LOADS OF VEG

1 large aubergine, cut into 2cm chunks

1 large sweet potato, peeled and cut into 2cm chunks (you'll need 500g)

3 small onions, cut into wedges

1 tsp smoked paprika

1 tbsp chopped fresh thyme

3 tbsp rapeseed oil

1 x 400g tin of Puy lentils, drained and rinsed

100g cherry tomatoes, halved

50g sun-dried tomatoes in oil, drained and cut into strips

2 tsp sherry or red wine vinegar

100g feta cheese

2 tbsp toasted pine nuts

40g wild rocket

sea salt and freshly ground black pepper

Sweet Potato and Aubergine Puy Lentil Bake Serves 4

This makes a wonderful warm salad, perfect for a warm sunny evening. If you prefer, you could replace the lentils with a pouch of any pre-cooked grain, such as spelt or pearl barley.

Preheat the oven to 200°C (400°F/gas mark 6).

Tip the aubergine, sweet potato and onions into a large roasting tin. Sprinkle over the smoked paprika and season generously, then scatter over the thyme and drizzle with the oil. Using your hands, mix until everything is evenly combined. Roast for 20 minutes.

Remove the roasting tin from the oven and fold in the lentils, cherry tomatoes and sun-dried tomatoes. Roast for another 15 minutes, until the tomatoes have started to break down and everything is piping hot.

Drizzle over the vinegar and crumble the feta cheese on top. Scatter over the pine nuts and rocket, then serve straight to the table.

20 MINS

 1 HR

 LOADS OF VEG

 FREEZER FRIENDLY

2 tbsp rapeseed oil

a knob of butter

1 small cauliflower, broken into small florets

350g potatoes, peeled and cut into cubes

1 large onion, sliced

750ml hot vegetable stock

a large pinch of saffron strands

3 tbsp korma curry paste

250g Greek yoghurt

500g basmati rice, well rinsed

100g fine green beans, halved

100g frozen peas

juice of 1 lemon

a good handful of fresh coriander leaves

1 x 100g packet of honey-roasted cashew nuts

sea salt and freshly ground black pepper

TO SERVE

poppadums

raita

Spiced Vegetable Biryani
Serves 4-6

This all-in-one vegetable rice dish is quick and easy to make. It's delicious served with ready-made poppadums and some raita, but if you can't find a ready-made raita in the supermarket, just use tzatziki and add a pinch of garam masala – it's basically the same.

Preheat the oven to 200°C (400°F/gas mark 6).

Put the oil and butter in a large roasting tin and pop in the oven for 2 minutes to melt the butter. Add the cauliflower, potatoes and onion, tossing quickly to coat evenly. Season generously and roast for 15 minutes, until just beginning to catch around the edges.

Meanwhile, put the stock in a large jug and whisk in the saffron and curry paste until evenly combined, then stir in the Greek yoghurt.

Remove the vegetables from the oven and stir in the rice, green beans and peas along with the stock mixture. Cover the tin tightly with a double layer of foil and bake for 30 minutes, until the rice is tender and all the liquid has been absorbed.

Sprinkle the lemon juice over the biryani, then tip out onto a large serving platter and gently fluff up the rice grains with a fork. Scatter over the coriander and cashew nuts. Serve with a pile of poppadums and a bowl of raita.

20 MINS

 45 MINS

 LOADS OF VEG

 FREEZER FRIENDLY

1 large aubergine, cut into 2.5cm chunks

1 red pepper, cut into 2cm chunks

1 yellow pepper, cut into 2cm chunks

1 large red onion, cut into 2cm chunks

2 small courgettes, trimmed and cut into 2cm chunks

3 tbsp rapeseed oil

4 tsp red wine or sherry vinegar

1 tsp caster sugar

2 garlic cloves, crushed

1 mild fresh red chilli, deseeded and finely chopped

2 x 200g packets of ready-made falafel

2 tbsp chopped fresh flat-leaf parsley

sea salt and freshly ground black pepper

TO SERVE

warm pittas

tomato salsa

hummus

Mediterranean Falafel Traybake
Serves 4

There is now a fabulous selection of ready-made falafel in supermarkets and convenience stores, many of them from Irish producers. Made from chickpeas, falafel are a good source of plant-based protein and are high in fibre too.

Preheat the oven to 200°C (400°F/gas mark 6).

Put the aubergine, peppers, red onion and courgettes in a large roasting tin and season generously. Drizzle over the oil and use your hands to mix everything together. Roast for 25 minutes, until the veg are tender and just beginning to catch around the edges, tossing once to ensure they cook evenly.

Meanwhile, put the vinegar in a small bowl and stir in the sugar until dissolved. Tip in the garlic and chilli and stir again to combine.

Remove the vegetables from the oven and drizzle over the garlic and chilli mixture, then toss to combine. Nestle in the falafel and roast for another 10–12 minutes, until the falafel are piping hot and the vegetables are nicely charred.

Scatter over the parsley and serve straight to the table with warm pitta and separate bowls of tomato salsa and hummus.

30 MINS

 1½ HRS

 LOADS OF VEG

 FREEZER FRIENDLY

500g waxy new potatoes (see the intro), unpeeled and cut into slices 3mm thick

1 yellow or green courgette, trimmed and cut into slices 5mm thick

4 garlic cloves, finely chopped

2 tsp chopped fresh oregano (or 1 tsp dried)

2 tsp chopped fresh rosemary (or 1 tsp dried)

4 tbsp olive or rapeseed oil, plus extra for drizzling

2 x 400g tins of chopped tomatoes

2 red onions, thinly sliced

a handful of fresh basil leaves

sea salt and freshly ground black pepper

TO SERVE

marinated feta

olives

Greek Roasted Vegetables
Serves 4

In Greece this is known as briam and to make it you'll need yellow waxy potatoes such as Charlotte, or any Cypriot varieties will also work well. I find that the organic potatoes tend to be waxy, so that section is a good place to start looking in the supermarket. Try to roughly match up their size to the courgettes to make them easier to layer up.

Preheat the oven to 200°C (400°F/gas mark 6).

Put the potatoes and courgette in a large bowl with the garlic, oregano and rosemary. Season generously and drizzle over the 4 tablespoons of oil, then toss to coat evenly.

Pour one tin of tomatoes into the bottom of a shallow round casserole dish that is about 23cm on the base and season with salt and pepper, stirring to combine. Arrange the potatoes, courgettes and red onions in alternating rows, starting at the outside of the dish and working your way into the middle. Stir the second tin of tomatoes into the bowl that you've mixed the vegetables in so that it picks up any residue, then spoon this over the top of the vegetables, using a spatula to get every bit.

Drizzle the vegetables with a little more oil, then cover tightly with foil and bake for 45 minutes. Remove the foil and roast for another 30–35 minutes, until the vegetables are softened and lightly charred and all the liquid has evaporated.

Scatter over some fresh basil leaves and serve straight to the table with separate bowls of feta and olives.

CHAPTER 2 MAKE AHEAD

20 MINS

 1 HR 40 MINS

 LOADS OF VEG

 SLOW COOKER FRIENDLY

❋ FREEZER FRIENDLY

2 tbsp rapeseed oil, plus extra for greasing

4 onions, thinly sliced (on a mandolin is best)

3 fresh thyme sprigs, leaves stripped, plus extra to garnish

4 confit duck legs

1.5kg potatoes, peeled and thinly sliced (on a mandolin is best)

500ml chicken stock

knob of butter

FOR THE CABBAGE

knob of butter

1 Savoy cabbage, trimmed, stalks removed and thinly sliced

sea salt and freshly ground black pepper

Duck Confit, Potato and Onion Pie Serves 4–6

This looks so impressive and the flavour is off the scale thanks to the succulent, delicious duck. I just adore Skeaghanore duck, known as West Cork Confit Duck Legs in the Simply Better Dunnes Stores range. Helena and Eugene Hickey use a white Pekin duck, which has a high meat yield and has surprisingly fewer calories than a chicken breast once you remove the fat, making them just perfect for this recipe.

Preheat the oven to 180°C (350°F/gas mark 4).

Heat the oil in a large frying pan over a medium heat. Sauté the onions and thyme for 10–15 minutes, until soft and just beginning to colour around the edges. Season to taste.

Remove the skin from the duck and discard. Take all the meat off the bones, then shred.

Layer the potatoes in a large baking dish with the onions and duck. Season each layer as you go and finish with an attractive overlapping layer of the potatoes. Pour over the stock and top with tiny pieces of butter.

Rub some foil with oil and place it, oil side down, over the dish and seal tight. Bake for 45 minutes, then remove the foil and press the potatoes down with a metal spatula. Bake for another 15–20 minutes, until the stock has all been absorbed and the potatoes are golden brown. Scatter over thyme leaves to garnish. Once cooked this pie can be cooled down, covered with cling film and kept in the fridge or frozen.

Just before you're ready to serve, prepare the cabbage. Heat a large frying pan over a medium to high heat. Add the butter with 1 tablespoon of water. Bring to the boil, then add the cabbage and a pinch of salt and toss constantly over a high heat. Cover for a few minutes, then toss again and season with pepper.

Tip into a bowl and serve straight to the table with the duck confit, potato and onion pie so everyone can help themselves.

30 MINS + CHILLING OVERNIGHT

 6 HRS

 LOADS OF VEG

 FREEZER FRIENDLY (MEAT)

2 tbsp fennel seeds

2 tsp chilli flakes

10 garlic cloves, peeled

25g fresh flat-leaf parsley, leaves picked

4 tbsp chopped fresh thyme

2 tbsp sea salt

1 tbsp rapeseed oil

4kg boneless pork belly and loin (see the intro)

200ml white wine

FOR THE ROOT VEGETABLES

5 carrots, peeled and quartered

5 small parsnips, peeled and quartered

1 celeriac, peeled and cut into 2cm cubes

1 small turnip, peeled and cut into 2cm cubes

1 tbsp honey

sea salt and freshly ground black pepper

Porchetta with Roasted Root Vegetables Serves 8–10

This Italian version of a hog roast, stuffed with garlic and aromatics, is the perfect celebration centrepiece. Ask your butcher for a rectangular piece of pork belly and a separate piece of pork loin that's the same size so that it can be rolled up inside.

Heat a frying pan over a medium heat and lightly toast the fennel seeds until aromatic. Add the chilli flakes and toss the pan constantly for another minute, then tip into a food processor. Add the garlic, parsley, thyme, salt and oil and blitz to a paste.

Using a sharp knife, score the pork belly flesh, then rub in the aromatic paste. Put the pork loin on top and roll it up tightly. Tie with butcher's string at 4cm intervals and leave to sit uncovered in the fridge overnight to dry out the skin or freeze.

Allow the meat to come back to room temperature. Preheat the oven to 160°C (325°F/gas mark 3).

Pat the pork with kitchen paper and put it on a rack in a roasting tin. Roast for 4 hours, then turn up the oven as high as it will go and roast for another 30 minutes, until the pork is tender and the crackling is crisp and golden brown. Remove the pork from the tin and loosely cover the porchetta with foil. Set aside.

Skim off the fat from the juices in the bottom of the tin, then put 2 tablespoons into another roasting tin (reserve the juices for gravy). Add all the root vegetables and toss to coat evenly, then season to taste. Put in the oven, increase the temperature to 200°C (400°F/gas mark 6) and roast for 35–40 minutes. Give the veg a good shake, drizzle over the honey and roast for another 10–15 minutes, until golden.

Meanwhile, put the roasting tin with the meat juices back on the hob over a medium heat. Pour in the wine, stir well and season to taste, then reduce to a gravy consistency.

When ready to serve, carve the porchetta into slices and put on plates with the vegetables and gravy. Any leftovers will freeze very well separately.

20 MINS + OVERNIGHT MARINATING

 3 HRS

 SLOW COOKER FRIENDLY

 FREEZER FRIENDLY (MEAT)

3 tbsp dark muscovado sugar

2 tbsp tomato ketchup or hot barbecue sauce

1 tbsp prepared English mustard

1 tbsp Worcestershire sauce

1 heaped tsp smoked paprika

2 racks of baby back pork ribs

FOR THE SALAD

4 corn on the cob

1 tbsp rapeseed oil

4 tbsp mayonnaise

1 tbsp soured cream

40g feta cheese, finely crumbled

finely grated rind and juice of 1 lime

15g fresh coriander, leaves picked

3 spring onions, thinly sliced

a good pinch of smoked paprika

sea salt and freshly ground black pepper

TO SERVE

jacket potatoes

Barbecue Pork Ribs with Charred Corn Salad Serves 4

Ask the butcher for baby back ribs, which are a shorter, curved cut near the backbone. If you don't get barbecue weather, simply preheat the oven to 220°C (425°F/ gas mark 7) and roast for 20–25 minutes on a foil-lined baking tray. The marinade, which doubles up as a basting sauce, is the perfect balance between sweet and savoury without smothering the flavour of the ribs.

Mix the sugar, ketchup or barbecue sauce, mustard, Worcestershire sauce and smoked paprika in a small bowl, then smear half onto the ribs that are in a shallow non-metallic dish. Cover with cling film and marinate in the fridge overnight or freeze. Refrigerate the remaining marinade.

Allow the ribs to come back up to room temperature. Preheat the oven to 150°C (300°F/gas mark 2).

Cover the dish with the ribs tightly with foil and cook for 2 hours, basting once or twice, until tender. Discard the foil and baste again, then roast for another 20–30 minutes, until the ribs are very tender but not falling off the bone.

Heat a barbecue to a medium-high heat. Remove the husks and silks from the corn and rub all over with the oil, then season to taste. Barbecue the corn for 18–20 minutes, turning occasionally, until tender and well charred.

Baste the ribs in the rest of the marinade and barbecue for 25–30 minutes, turning once, until crisp and lightly charred. The cooked ribs can also be frozen.

Cut the corn kernels from the cobs into a bowl. Put the mayonnaise, soured cream, feta, lime rind and juice in a bowl and season to taste. Whisk until smooth.

Spoon half of the corn onto a serving platter and drizzle half of the crema over the top. Sprinkle with half of the coriander, spring onions and paprika. Repeat with the rest of the of the ingredients.

Serve the ribs on a chopping board with the charred corn salad and jacket potatoes.

20 MINS

 2 HRS

 SLOW COOKER FRIENDLY

❋ FREEZER FRIENDLY

1 tbsp rapeseed oil

450g premium pork sausages

2 onions, sliced

150g dry-cured bacon lardons

1 tbsp plain flour

2 tsp fresh thyme leaves

4 carrots, sliced

750g potatoes, peeled and thinly sliced

2 tsp Worcestershire sauce

400ml chicken stock

15g butter

1 tbsp chopped fresh flat-leaf parsley

sea salt and freshly ground black pepper

Dublin Coddle
Serves 4–6

As a Cavan man I can't pretend that this is an authentic version (I like to brown the sausages first so that they have a bit of colour), but I can promise that it's tasty and easy to make. There are now so many delicious premium sausages on the market, but I love Pat O'Neill's range from Wexford. He also does excellent lardons, which are just thick-cut pieces of streaky bacon with all the work done for you!

Preheat the oven to 180°C (350°F/gas mark 4).

Heat half of the oil in an ovenproof sauté pan or casserole dish. Brown the sausages for 3–4 minutes, turning regularly. Transfer to a chopping board and cut each one into three pieces. Set aside.

Add the rest of the oil to the pan and sauté the onions and bacon for 6–8 minutes, until lightly golden. Stir in the flour and thyme and cook for 1 minute, stirring. Tip in the sausage pieces, the carrots and half of the potatoes. Season generously, then shake the pan to get everything into an even layer.

Turn off the heat and arrange the rest of the potatoes on top in a nice overlapping layer. Stir the Worcestershire sauce into the stock, then pour this over the potatoes. Dot with butter and season to taste.

Cover with a lid and bake for 1 hour, then remove the lid and cook for another 30 minutes, until the potato topping is tender and golden brown.

Scatter over the parsley and serve straight to the table or freeze.

20 MINS

 2 HRS

 SLOW COOKER FRIENDLY

❄ FREEZER FRIENDLY (PORK BELLY)

2 garlic cloves, crushed

2 tbsp freshly grated root ginger

4 tbsp hoisin sauce

3 tbsp soy sauce

3 tbsp honey

3 tbsp dark muscovado sugar

2 tbsp rice wine vinegar

500g rindless pork belly slices, cut into 7.5cm pieces

FOR THE PICKLED VEGETABLES

200ml rice wine vinegar

1 tbsp caster sugar

1 tsp sea salt

2 red onions, thinly sliced

1 large carrot, julienned

100g radishes, trimmed and thinly sliced

TO SERVE

2 tbsp mayonnaise

1 tsp wasabi

4–6 brioche buns, lightly toasted

50g soft lettuce leaves

Crispy Hoisin Pork Belly Brioche Buns Serves 4–6

Melt-in-the-mouth pork belly in a sticky hoisin barbecue sauce is perfect for filling soft brioche buns with some pickled vegetables to cut through the richness. The pickled vegetables will last up to two weeks in a sterilised jar in the fridge.

Preheat the oven to 160°C (325°F/gas mark 3).

Mix the garlic, ginger, hoisin, soy, honey, muscovado and vinegar in a bowl. Put 4 tablespoons of the marinade into a small casserole and pour in 50ml of water, stirring to combine. Add the pork belly pieces, then cover with a lid and cook for 1½ hours, until very tender. This can be frozen at this point.

To prepare the pickled vegetables, put the vinegar, caster sugar and salt in a pan and bring to a simmer. Put the onions, carrot and radishes in a colander and pour over a kettle of just-boiled water. Drain well and tip into a bowl, then pour over the warm vinegar and set aside until needed, stirring occasionally to ensure they pickle evenly. This can be made in advance and kept in a sterilised container in the fridge for up to two weeks.

Preheat the grill to its highest setting. Arrange the cooked pork belly strips on a large baking sheet lined with foil. Baste with the rest of the marinade and grill for 3–4 minutes, turning halfway through and brushing with the sauce from the tin, until the sauce is thick and sticky and the slices are nicely charred. This can be frozen at this point.

To serve, mix the mayonnaise with the wasabi, then spread this over the bottoms of the buns. Add a pile of the lettuce leaves, then top with the hoisin pork and drained pickled vegetables. Finish with the brioche bun tops.

20 MINS

 1½ HRS

 SLOW COOKER FRIENDLY

 FREEZER FRIENDLY

1 tbsp rapeseed oil

1 large onion, finely chopped

2 celery sticks, finely chopped

100g chestnut button mushrooms, sliced

400g lean minced beef

800g passata (or 2 x 400g jars of pasta sauce)

a good pinch of caster sugar

225g penne pasta

100g ball of mozzarella, cut into cubes

50g mature Cheddar cheese, finely grated

sea salt and freshly ground black pepper

TO SERVE

dressed green salad

Bolognese Pasta Bake
Serves 4

This all-in-one pasta Bolognese is packed with flavour and can be made well in advance, ready to pop in the oven. I like to serve it with a lovely big soft leaf salad. It's something we often make at home and everyone happily tucks in.

Heat the oil in a sauté pan over a high heat. Add the onion, celery and mushrooms and fry for about 3 minutes, until softened. Add the mince and quickly brown, breaking up the lumps with a wooden spoon. Stir in the passata or pasta sauce and sugar, then season to taste. Cover and simmer for 45 minutes, stirring once or twice, until tender.

Preheat the oven to 160°C (325°F/gas mark 3).

Cook the pasta in boiling salted water for 8–10 minutes, until tender but still with a little bite. Drain well, then stir into the mince.

Spoon the Bolognese mixture into an ovenproof dish and sprinkle over both cheeses. This can be stored in the fridge or frozen at this point. Bake for 25–30 minutes, until golden and bubbling around the edges.

Serve straight to the table with a big bowl of salad on the side.

20 MINS

 2 HRS 20 MINS

 SLOW COOKER FRIENDLY

 FREEZER FRIENDLY (MEAT)

2 tbsp rapeseed oil, plus extra for brushing

800g braising steak, trimmed and cut into 3cm slices

400ml beef stock

25g butter

3 large onions, sliced

2 garlic cloves, finely chopped

1 tbsp light muscovado sugar

2 tsp fresh thyme leaves, plus extra to garnish

2 tbsp plain flour

300ml white wine

FOR THE CROÛTES

1 sourdough baguette (about 30cm long)

2 large eggs

3 tbsp crème fraîche

1 tbsp Dijon mustard

175g Gruyère cheese, finely grated

sea salt and freshly ground black pepper

TO SERVE

steamed French beans (optional)

Beef Stew with Gruyère Croûtes
Serves 4–6

This delicious stew is elevated to new heights with the addition of the cheesy croûtes. It's a perfect dish if you find yourself looking for something special for a midweek meal if you want to be well organised in advance. Simply reheat the stew gently on the hob and add the croûtes before popping into the oven.

Heat half of the oil in a casserole over a high heat. Tip in the beef, season generously and sauté until browned. Transfer to a bowl. Add a little of the stock to deglaze the casserole, then pour into the bowl.

Add the rest of the oil to the casserole with half of the butter. Tip in the onions and a good pinch of salt. Sauté for 8–10 minutes, stirring regularly, until starting to brown. Stir in the rest of the butter with the garlic, sugar and thyme, then reduce the heat to low and cook the onions for another 30 minutes, stirring occasionally, until caramelised. Set aside a large spoonful for garnish.

Meanwhile, preheat the oven to 180°C (350°F/gas mark 4).

Cut the baguette into 12 x 2cm-thick slices, discarding the ends. Brush with oil on both sides and season. Arrange on a baking sheet and bake for 5–8 minutes, turning after 5 minutes, until crisp.

Increase the heat under the casserole to medium. Stir the flour into the onions and cook for 1 minute, then stir in the wine and allow it to bubble down for a minute or two. Pour in the rest of the stock and tip in the browned beef mix, stirring to combine. Bring to a simmer and cook for 1½ hours, until the beef is meltingly tender. This can be made in advance or frozen at this stage.

To prepare the croûtes, mix the eggs, crème fraîche and mustard in a bowl, then season and stir in the Gruyère. When the beef is tender, remove the casserole from the oven and increase the heat to 200°C (400°F/gas mark 6). Spread the topping on the croûtes, then arrange them on top of the beef. Bake for another 15–20 minutes, until golden brown and bubbling.

Scatter over the reserved caramelised onions and a few thyme leaves and serve straight to the table with a bowl of steamed French beans, if liked.

20 MINS

 4 HRS

 SLOW COOKER FRIENDLY

 FREEZER FRIENDLY

1.75kg beef brisket

2 tbsp rapeseed oil

a knob of butter

6 red onions, cut into wedges

500ml beef stock

120ml balsamic vinegar

4 tbsp honey

1 tbsp soy sauce

4 garlic cloves, finely chopped

1 tbsp chopped fresh thyme

3 tbsp cornflour

sea salt and freshly ground black pepper

TO SERVE

mashed potatoes

steamed cavolo nero

steamed baby carrots

Sticky Balsamic Beef Brisket
Serves 12

This is very simple to batch cook and the extra portions can be frozen for a later date. I've suggested serving it with some creamy mash, but it would also be delicious with jacket potatoes, polenta or rice to mix things up. The brisket runs from the bottom of the neck down under the ribs. Cut from the breast, this braising cut is excellent value in your local butcher and must be cooked slow and low.

Preheat the oven to 160°C (325°F/gas mark 3).

Dry the brisket with kitchen paper and season generously. Heat half of the oil in a casserole over a high heat and brown all over for about 5 minutes. Transfer to a plate.

Add the rest of the oil to the casserole with the butter and sauté the onions for 6–8 minutes, until they are starting to colour. Transfer to a bowl and set aside.

Put the stock in a jug and whisk in the balsamic, honey, soy, garlic and thyme. Put the brisket back into the casserole and pour over the stock mixture. Cover and cook for 2 hours, then remove from the oven and add the onions. Cover again and cook for another 1½ hours, until the beef is meltingly tender.

Carefully lift out the brisket and transfer it to a board. Snip the string and use two forks to shred the meat, discarding any fatty bits. Put the cornflour in a small bowl and stir in 2–3 tablespoons of water until you have a smooth paste. Whisk this into the liquid in the casserole, then stir in the shredded beef. Bring to a simmer over a low heat and cook for a few minutes to thicken the sauce slightly.

Serve the sticky balsamic beef in wide-rimmed bowls with some mashed potatoes, cavolo nero and baby carrots. Freeze the extra portions.

25 MINS

 1 HR 45 MINS

 SLOW COOKER FRIENDLY

 FREEZER FRIENDLY

2 tbsp rapeseed oil

50g butter

4 large onions, thinly sliced

2 tbsp light muscovado sugar

1 tbsp fresh thyme leaves

400g lamb mince

2 celery sticks, diced

2 carrots, diced

1 garlic clove, crushed

1 heaped tbsp plain flour

1 tbsp Worcestershire sauce

2 tsp tomato purée

200ml white wine

300ml chicken stock

1kg potatoes, peeled

4 tbsp milk

50g mature Cheddar cheese, finely grated

sea salt and freshly ground black pepper

TO SERVE

buttered petit pois

French Onion Shepherd's Pie
Serves 4-6

Here I'm taking a firm family favourite to next-level cooking. To get the true flavour of the caramelised onions for this pie, expect them to take a bit of time, but you will be rewarded with the melting texture and deep colour that are required. I love to use Connemara Hill lamb, it's well worth seeking out.

To caramelise the onions, heat half of the oil and half of the butter in a large heavy-based frying pan over a medium to high heat. Stir in the onions with a pinch of salt and sauté for 8–10 minutes, until starting to brown. Sprinkle in the sugar and thyme, then reduce the heat to low and cook for about 45 minutes, stirring occasionally.

Meanwhile, heat the rest of the oil in a casserole over a medium to high heat and sauté the mince until well browned, breaking it up with a wooden spoon. Using a slotted spoon, transfer to a bowl. Set aside.

Reduce the heat, tip in the celery and carrots and sauté for 8–10 minutes. Stir in the garlic, then mix in the flour, Worcestershire sauce and tomato purée and cook for another 2 minutes, stirring. Return the mince to the casserole, pour in the wine and reduce by half. Add the stock and season generously, then bring to a simmer and cook, uncovered, for 45 minutes, until the liquid has reduced to a gravy.

Put the potatoes in a pan of boiling salted water and cook for about 20 minutes, until tender. Drain well and leave to steam dry for a couple of minutes, then mash well. Beat in the rest of the butter with the milk, then stir in the cheese.

Stir the caramelised onions into the lamb mixture, which should be ready at this point, and season to taste. Transfer to a suitable ovenproof dish and cover with the mashed potatoes. This can be made in advance or frozen at this stage.

Preheat the oven to 200°C (400°F/gas mark 6).

Place the dish on a baking tray and cook for 30–45 minutes, until bubbling and golden brown. The cooking time will depend on whether it has been chilled down first. Serve with the petit pois.

20 MINS + MARINATE OVERNIGHT

 4 HRS 30 MINS

 SLOW COOKER FRIENDLY (LAMB)

 FREEZER FRIENDLY

2kg lamb shoulder

4 tbsp dried harissa spice seasoning

1 tbsp rapeseed oil

1 x 290g jar of grilled mixed peppers in olive oil

2 garlic cloves, peeled

3 tbsp sherry vinegar

1 tsp smoked paprika

sea salt and freshly ground black pepper

TO SERVE

8–10 Mediterranean olive oil wraps

100g wild rocket or baby salad leaves

1 x 200g carton of tzatziki

Pulled Harissa Lamb
Serves 8–10

This recipe uses a small lamb shoulder, which is such a great-value cut. I find that we always get two dinners out of it, so once it's been cooked, I'll freeze the leftovers for another day – always a bonus.

Make small cuts all over the lamb, place in a suitable non-metallic container and rub the harissa all over it, getting right into the cuts. Cover with cling film and marinate in the fridge overnight. This can be made well in advance or frozen at this stage.

Preheat the oven to 150°C (300°F/gas mark 2).

Put the lamb into a snug-fitting roasting tin and smear it again with any harissa that has dripped off, then rub all over with the oil and season generously. Add a splash of water to the tin, then roast for 4 hours, until the meat is tender and easily falls away from the bone.

Drain the peppers (reserve the oil) and put into a food processor with the garlic, vinegar and smoked paprika. Season generously and pulse to a purée, then add enough of the oil through the feeder tube to make a smooth dressing. Transfer to a clean jar and set aside until needed or this will keep in the fridge for up to one week.

Remove the lamb from the oven and transfer to a large platter. Using two forks, take all the meat and crispy skin off the bone and roughly chop, discarding the bone. Skim away any excess fat from the tin, then add another splash of boiling water. Stir it around to pick up all the sticky juices from the bottom, then fold into the meat. Cover loosely with foil and keep in a low oven until ready to serve or take it out and chill or freeze for another day.

Heat the wraps according to the packet instructions. Serve the shredded lamb on a platter with the roasted pepper dressing with the salad leaves and tzatziki in bowls alongside.

1 HR

 6 HRS

 SLOW COOKER FRIENDLY

✿ FREEZER FRIENDLY

2 large red onions, thickly sliced into rounds

3 tbsp rapeseed oil

1 cinnamon stick

2 tsp dried oregano

1 tsp ground cumin

1 tsp ground coriander

1 tsp paprika

4 garlic cloves, peeled

2 tsp sea salt

15g fresh mint, leaves stripped

rind and juice of 1 clementine

4 tbsp honey

2.25kg leg of lamb on the bone

300ml chicken stock

1 x 100g packet of pomegranate seeds

freshly ground black pepper

TO SERVE

couscous

Spiced Pomegranate Slow-Roast Leg of Lamb Serves 8–10

This recipe yields plenty of meat and as it can be made in advance, it's perfect for getting ahead at the weekend. The trick is to roast the lamb in a large tent of foil, creating enough space over the lamb so that the foil is in no danger of sticking to the meat and so that steam can circulate inside the tent. The resulting texture is half-roasted, half-pulled, fork-tender lamb that's very easy to shred.

Put the onions in a roasting tin, toss in 2 tablespoons of the oil and tuck in the cinnamon stick.

Put the oregano in a mini blender with the cumin, coriander, paprika, garlic, salt, mint (reserving a little to garnish) and clementine rind and juice and blitz to a purée. Transfer to a bowl and stir in the remaining oil and the honey to make a paste.

Lightly score the lamb with diagonal incisions and sit it on the onion trivet in the roasting tin. Rub all over with the paste and season with pepper. Give it 45 minutes to come up to room temperature (or marinate in the fridge overnight if time allows).

Preheat the oven to 160°C (325°F/gas mark 3) and remove the top shelf.

Pour the stock around the lamb and cover with two large pieces of tin foil to make a large tent, pinching the foil securely. Put the tin on the bottom shelf of the oven and roast for 5 hours, basting twice and ensuring that the foil is tightly sealed up again afterwards.

Increase the heat to 180°C (350°F/gas mark 4) and roast for another 40 minutes, then remove the foil, baste again and cook for 20 minutes, until the lamb is falling off the bone. Cover again with the foil and leave to rest for 20 minutes. If you want to get ahead, shred the meat at this point and chill or freeze.

To serve, transfer the lamb and onions on to a serving platter with the couscous and scatter over the pomegranate seeds and reserved mint leaves.

30 MINS

 40 MINS

 SLOW COOKER FRIENDLY

 FREEZER FRIENDLY

40g butter

2 large garlic cloves, finely chopped

100g button mushrooms, thinly sliced

3 tbsp plain flour

600ml milk

100g cream cheese

50g freshly grated Parmesan cheese

150g baby spinach leaves

1 large egg

250g ricotta cheese

1 tbsp chopped fresh flat-leaf parsley

8 large no-cook lasagne sheets

400g cooked chicken, cut into bite-sized pieces or shredded

200g grated mozzarella cheese

sea salt and freshly grated black pepper

TO SERVE

dressed green salad

Chicken and Spinach Lasagne
Serves 6–8

This recipe is perfect for batch cooking by simply doubling the ingredients or making individual lasagnes. Alternatively, make this on a Sunday with the leftovers from your roast and keep it in the fridge for up to three days for a hassle-free meal. It's also an excellent way to use a rotisserie chicken, which most supermarkets are selling now.

Preheat the oven to 200°C (400°F/gas mark 6).

Melt the butter in a pan over a medium heat and stir in the garlic and mushrooms. Season to taste and sauté for 2–3 minutes, until the mushrooms are tender. Sprinkle over the flour and cook for 1 minute, stirring. Gradually whisk in the milk and season generously. Bring to a simmer, then reduce the heat and cook for a few minutes, until thickened. Whisk in the cream cheese and half of the Parmesan, then remove from the heat and stir in the spinach until wilted.

Whisk the egg, ricotta and parsley in a bowl and season generously.

Spoon one-quarter of the sauce into a lasagne dish. Cover with two of the lasagne sheets. Add one-third of the ricotta mix, then add one-third of the chicken, half of the mozzarella and sprinkle with a little of the remaining Parmesan. Repeat these layers twice more, then finish with the last two lasagne sheets and the rest of the sauce and Parmesan. This can be made in advance or frozen at this stage.

Bake for 25 minutes, until bubbling and golden brown. Leave to settle before cutting into slices and serving on plates with salad.

20 MINS + MARINATING

 30 MINS

 LOADS OF VEG

 FREEZER FRIENDLY (CHICKEN)

Korean-Style Glazed Chicken with Pickled Baby Vegetables
Serves 4–6

4 garlic cloves, crushed

1 tbsp freshly grated root ginger

120ml soy sauce

3 tbsp gochujang (see the intro)

2 tbsp rice wine vinegar

50g light muscovado sugar

500g skinless, boneless chicken thighs

1 tsp sesame seeds

FOR THE PICKLED BABY VEGETABLES

1 red onion

1 x 200g packet of baby cucumbers

1 x 250g packet of baby carrots

100g radishes

1 tbsp caster sugar

1 tsp sea salt

200ml rice wine vinegar

TO SERVE

jasmine rice or bao buns

Korean food is packed full of punchy flavours and this recipe a great way to give it a try. Gochujang is a Korean chilli paste made from chilli powder, fermented soybeans, glutinous rice and salt. It has a unique spicy kick and is well worth seeking out – any Asian market should have it. However, if you can't find it, use equal quantities of tomato ketchup and sriracha chilli sauce for a slightly different flavour that is still delicious. If you do make a trip to an Asian market, pick up some bao buns to serve with this instead of the rice.

For the marinade, whisk together the garlic, ginger, soy sauce, gochujang, rice wine vinegar and muscovado sugar, then stir in the chicken to coat. Cover with cling film and leave to marinate in the fridge for at least 2 hours or overnight is ideal. This can also be made well in advance or frozen at this stage.

Cut the red onion, cucumbers, carrots and radishes into thin slices and put in a bowl. Sprinkle over the caster sugar and salt, then add the vinegar, stirring to combine. Set aside in the fridge for 20 minutes (or up to one month in the fridge if the vegetables are submerged in liquid).

Preheat the oven to 190°C (375°F/gas mark 5).

Remove the chicken from the marinade and arrange on a foil-lined baking sheet. Pour the marinade into a small pan. Roast the chicken for 20 minutes.

Meanwhile, simmer the marinade over a low heat until thickened, whisking occasionally. Do not allow it to boil. Remove the chicken from the oven and brush with the glaze, then roast for another 5 minutes, until tender and slightly caramelised. Remove from the oven and brush with another coat of the glaze, then scatter over the sesame seeds.

Cut the chicken into slices and serve with the pickled veg and jasmine rice or in bao buns.

30 MINS + MARINATING

 30 MINS

 LOADS OF VEG

❀ FREEZER FRIENDLY (CHICKEN AND SAUCE)

2 large chicken fillets

250ml buttermilk

4 tsp medium curry powder

100g panko breadcrumbs

vegetable oil, for frying

1 onion, finely chopped

1 carrot, finely chopped

2 garlic cloves, grated

5cm piece of fresh root ginger, peeled and grated

1 tsp ground turmeric

1 tbsp plain flour

300ml chicken stock

1 x 160ml can of coconut cream

1 tsp caster sugar

1 tsp soy sauce

FOR THE SALAD

200g red cabbage, shredded

1 large carrot, julienned

1 tsp caster sugar

2 tbsp rice wine vinegar

sea salt and freshly ground black pepper

TO SERVE

jasmine rice

thinly sliced spring onions

toasted sesame seeds

Katsu Chicken Curry
Serves 4

Japan's most popular dish is easy to scale up if you fancy making multiple portions.

Cut the chicken in half lengthways. Place each one between two sheets of parchment paper and beat with a rolling pin to even out the thickness.

Pour the buttermilk, half of the curry powder and a pinch of salt in a bowl, then add the chicken. Cover with cling film and leave in the fridge for at least 20 minutes or overnight is ideal.

To make the sauce, heat a little oil in a frying pan over a medium to low heat. Add the onion, carrot, garlic and ginger and sauté for about 10 minutes. Stir in the remaining curry powder and the turmeric and cook for 1 minute, then stir in the flour and continue to cook for a minute or two, stirring.

Pour the stock into the vegetables, stirring continuously, then stir in the coconut cream, sugar and soy. Simmer for another 6–8 minutes, until slightly reduced, then blitz with a hand-held blender until smooth. This can be made in advance or frozen at this stage.

Meanwhile, to make the salad, toss the cabbage and carrot in a bowl with a good pinch of salt and the sugar and vinegar. Set aside for at least 10 minutes or up to three days in the fridge is fine.

Take the chicken out of the buttermilk and shake off any excess, then put it in the breadcrumbs, pressing them down to help them stick. Put back on a plate and chill until needed. This can also be made in advance up to this point or frozen at this stage.

Heat a large frying pan over a medium to high heat and add a thin layer of vegetable oil. Working in batches, add the chicken and fry for 3–4 minutes on each side, until crisp and deep golden.

To serve, cut the chicken into strips and arrange on plates with some jasmine rice and salad, then spoon the sauce over the chicken. Garnish with spring onions and toasted sesame seeds.

20 MINS + 1 HR MARINATING

 20 MINS

 FREEZER FRIENDLY (CHICKEN)

200ml buttermilk

300g mini chicken fillets

100g panko breadcrumbs

25g plain flour

1 tsp paprika

2 eggs

4 tbsp rapeseed oil

sea salt and freshly ground black pepper

TO SERVE

2 tbsp snipped fresh chives

100g soured cream

8 small wraps

2 Little Gem lettuces, cut into thin wedges

4 spring onions, very thinly sliced

hot chilli sauce

Buttermilk Chicken Tender Wraps Serves 4

These taste so much better than any shop-bought version and are actually very easy to prepare. You can use chicken breast fillets cut into strips or boneless, skinless chicken thighs cut into quarters for this recipe, but the mini fillets are the perfect size. The same technique works with pork steak cut into thin slices. This recipe is worth doubling so that you can freeze what you need for another day.

Pour the buttermilk into a bowl and season generously, then stir in the chicken. Cover with cling film and marinate in the fridge for 1 hour.

Heat a large non-stick frying pan. Tip in the breadcrumbs and toast in the dry pan for 2–3 minutes, stirring regularly to ensure they don't burn, until lightly golden. Tip into a shallow dish, breaking up any clumps with your fingers.

Put the flour and paprika on a plate and mix to combine. Break the eggs into a bowl and season, then whisk lightly. Lift the chicken fillets out of the buttermilk, shaking off any excess, then toss them in the flour. Quickly dip into the beaten eggs, then roll in the breadcrumbs. Arrange on a baking sheet lined with parchment paper. These can be made well in advance or frozen at this stage.

Preheat the oven to 220°C (425°F/gas mark 7).

Heat half of the oil in the frying pan over a medium to low heat. Add half of the chicken and cook for 1–2 minutes on each side, until crisp and lightly golden. Put back on the baking sheet and use the rest of the oil to fry the rest, then cook the chicken in the oven for 5 minutes, until cooked through and golden brown. Slice each chicken piece in half diagonally.

Stir half of the chives into the soured cream and season to taste. Warm the wraps in the microwave or on a pan according to the packet instructions.

Serve the warm wraps topped with the chicken, lettuce wedges, a dollop of the soured cream, the spring onions and a generous drizzle of the hot chilli sauce, then scatter over the remaining chives.

45 MINS

 50 MINS

 LOADS OF VEG

✲ FREEZER FRIENDLY

8 large chicken thighs, bone in and skin on

100g mango chutney

1 tbsp lemon juice

1 tsp cumin seeds

FOR THE PULAO

500g basmati rice

50g butter

2 cardamom pods, lightly crushed

1 tsp cumin seeds

3 bay leaves

3 mild fresh green chillies, stalks snapped off

1 large onion, finely chopped

1 waxy potato, cut into 1cm dice

2 carrots, cut into 1cm dice

100g green beans, cut into 2.5cm lengths

150g frozen petit pois

750ml light vegetable stock

2 tbsp lemon juice

a good handful of fresh coriander, finely chopped

sea salt and freshly ground black pepper

Mango Chutney Chicken with Vegetable Pulao Serves 6-8

This is a great dish to make and return to later in the week or it could be frozen, although you'll lose the delicious crispy chicken skin. It's made from ingredients from the store cupboard and some basic veg, but you can be as imaginative as you like depending on what you have.

Wash the rice in a sieve until the water runs clear, then soak in a bowl of cold water for 30 minutes.

Preheat the oven to 200°C (400°F/gas mark 6).

Arrange the chicken in a baking tin lined with parchment paper. Mix the mango chutney with the lemon juice and cumin seeds in a small bowl and season generously, then spoon over the chicken. Roast for 35–40 minutes, until the chicken thighs are tender and nicely caramelised.

To make the pulao, melt the butter in a casserole or heavy-based pan with a lid over a low heat. Add the cardamom, cumin seeds, bay leaves and chillies and sauté for 30 seconds. Tip in the onion and cook until it's just beginning to brown around the edges. Add the potato and carrots and sauté for another 8–10 minutes, until the potato is just cooked.

Drain the soaked rice and add it to the pan. Stir in the green beans and petit pois and season generously with salt and pepper, then add the stock and lemon juice, stirring to combine.

Cover the pulao with a tight-fitting lid and cook for 10–12 minutes, until the rice is just tender and all the liquid has been absorbed. Remove from the heat and leave to settle for 10 minutes with the lid still on. Keep extra portions in the fridge or freeze at this stage.

Just before serving, fork the coriander through the rice and arrange the vegetable pulao on plates with the chicken thighs.

30 MINS

 1 HR

 LOADS OF VEG

 FREEZER FRIENDLY (CHICKEN AND RICE)

1 tbsp rapeseed oil

500g chicken fillets or skinless, boneless thighs, diced

1 tbsp soy sauce

1 tsp sesame oil

FOR THE SATAY SAUCE

75ml boiling water

6 tbsp crunchy peanut butter

juice of ½ lime

3 tbsp soy sauce

1 tbsp sweet chilli sauce

1 tsp light muscovado sugar

FOR THE SALAD

300g short grain brown rice

150g edamame beans

1 small head of broccoli, cut into bite-sized florets

1 small ripe mango, peeled and diced (or use a carton of ready-prepared)

6 radishes, thinly sliced

2 carrots, julienned

3 spring onions, finely sliced

2 tsp toasted black sesame seeds

sea salt and freshly ground black pepper

Chicken Satay Bowls
Serves 4-6

This is a great recipe to make ahead for meal prep so that you can eat it over the next couple of days, hot or cold. There are no rules when it comes to salads like this, so use whatever veggies you have in the fridge that you think will marry well with the satay sauce. You could also change the chicken for beef, lamb or tofu. If you are making these bowls ahead of time, leave all the elements to cool and store them separately in airtight containers in the fridge until needed.

To cook the rice, rinse it well under cold running water, then put it in a pan with a tight-fitting lid with a good pinch of salt. Pour in 600ml of water and bring to the boil, then reduce the heat and simmer very gently for 50 minutes without disturbing it. Remove the pan from the heat and set aside for another 10 minutes without lifting the lid. Fluff up the rice with a fork.

Heat the rapeseed oil in a non-stick frying pan over a medium to high heat. Add the chicken and season generously, then sauté for 4–5 minutes, until cooked through and lightly golden. Drizzle over the soy sauce and sesame oil and continue tossing until the chicken is coated and all the liquid has evaporated.

Blanch the edamame beans and broccoli for 2–3 minutes in a pan of boiling salted water. Drain and refresh under cold running water, then drain on kitchen paper.

To make the satay sauce, pour the boiling water into a bowl and add the peanut butter. Stir until smooth, then stir in the lime juice, soy sauce, sweet chilli sauce and sugar.

To assemble, divide the hot or cold rice between bowls, then arrange the chicken, edamame beans, broccoli, mango, radishes, carrots and spring onions on top. Scatter over the sesame seeds and drizzle over the hot or cold satay sauce to serve.

20 MINS

 30 MINS

 FREEZER FRIENDLY

Turkey Meatballs with Grilled Mixed Pepper Sauce Serves 4–6

100g sweetcorn kernels (fresh, frozen or canned)

2 tbsp milk

100g fresh white breadcrumbs

4 spring onions, very finely chopped

1 garlic clove, crushed

2 tbsp chopped fresh flat-leaf parsley, plus extra to garnish

2 tsp ground cumin

1 tsp garam masala

1 egg, beaten

500g turkey mince

sunflower oil, for frying

FOR THE SAUCE

1 x 400g jar or tin of grilled mixed peppers

3 tbsp rapeseed oil

20g fresh coriander, roughly chopped

1 garlic clove, peeled

2 tbsp apple cider vinegar

2 tbsp sweet chilli sauce

sea salt and freshly ground black pepper

TO SERVE

couscous

I've added some charred sweetcorn to these moreish meatballs. They're light and succulent, but be very gentle when it comes to mixing the mince and forming meatballs or they might get rubbery. This is why I like to mix everything else together thoroughly before adding the turkey, then knead the mince into the rest of the ingredients until just combined. Make a double batch – half for dinner and half to be frozen.

To make the meatballs, heat a large non-stick frying pan over a high heat and sauté the sweetcorn for 2–3 minutes, until lightly blackened. Tip into a bowl and leave for a few minutes to cool down. Sprinkle the milk over the breadcrumbs and allow to soften, then add the charred sweetcorn along with the spring onions, garlic, parsley, cumin, garam masala and egg. Season generously and mix well, then gently mix in the turkey mince (see the intro) and shape into 20 walnut-sized meatballs. Keep extra portions in the fridge or freeze at this stage.

To make the grilled mixed pepper sauce, drain the peppers and rinse well under the tap, then quickly dry on kitchen paper. Put into a food processor with the oil, coriander, garlic, vinegar and sweet chilli sauce. Season generously with salt and blitz until smooth, then season again to taste. Transfer to a suitable container and set aside until needed. Keep extra portions in the fridge or freeze at this stage.

Preheat the oven to 200°C (400°F/gas mark 6).

Heat a layer of sunflower oil in the frying pan and sauté the meatballs in batches for about 5 minutes, turning them regularly with tongs, until golden brown all over. Transfer to a baking tin. Finish cooking the meatballs in the oven for 5 minutes, until cooked through and golden brown.

To serve, arrange on plates with couscous and drizzle over the grilled mixed pepper sauce, then garnish with the extra parsley.

20 MINS + MARINATING

 1 HR

 FREEZER FRIENDLY (CHICKEN)

Chicken Kebabs
Serves 8

150g natural yoghurt

juice of 1 lemon

1 tbsp peanut butter

4 garlic cloves, peeled

5cm piece of fresh root ginger, peeled and roughly chopped

20g fresh coriander, plus extra to garnish

1 fresh green chilli

1 tsp ground cumin

1 tsp garam masala

½ tsp ground turmeric

16 boneless, skinless chicken thighs, cut into 4cm pieces

2 red peppers, cut into 4cm pieces

2 yellow peppers, cut into 4cm pieces

2 red onions, cut into 4cm pieces

2 tbsp rapeseed oil

sea salt and freshly ground black pepper

TO SERVE

8 mini naan or flatbreads

spiced mango chutney

tzatziki

a handful of fresh mint leaves

These kebabs are packed full of flavour. For ease I've given instructions to cook them in the oven, but of course they would also be delicious cooked on the barbecue. The chicken can be left marinating for up to three days and the flavour only gets better, so you could get two days out of this recipe or you could freeze the chicken for another day.

Put the yoghurt into a mini blender or NutriBullet with the lemon juice, peanut butter, garlic, ginger, coriander, green chilli, cumin, garam masala and turmeric. Season generously and blitz to a smooth paste, then put the chicken in a bowl and stir in the yoghurt mixture until evenly coated. Cover and marinate in the fridge for at least 4 hours, but up to three days is good – the longer, the better. The chicken can also be frozen at this stage.

Preheat the oven to 220°C (425°F/gas mark 7). Line the base of a roasting tin with parchment paper.

Put the peppers and onions in the lined roasting tin, then toss in the oil and season generously. Roast for 25 minutes, until the vegetables are beginning to char around the edges.

Thread the chicken onto 16 x 20cm soaked bamboo (or metal) skewers and arrange on a wire rack that will sit on top of the roasting tin that the vegetables are in. Remove the vegetables from the oven and give them a good stir. Put the wire rack with the kebabs on top into the tin and return to the oven for 20 minutes, until the chicken is cooked through and tender and the vegetables are nicely charred but not burned. Remove from the oven and leave to rest in a warm place.

Arrange the naan or flatbreads on baking sheets and cook in the oven for 5 minutes (or according to the packet instructions) to heat through.

To serve, arrange the chicken kebabs on plates with the naan or flatbreads and some roasted vegetables. Add dollops of mango chutney and tzatziki and garnish with coriander and mint leaves.

20 MINS

 1 HR

FREEZER FRIENDLY (BURGERS)

Tuna Melt Burgers
Makes 4

These nifty burgers are perfect if you want to double the recipe or get ahead with your prep. However, they can also be made in less than half an hour from store cupboard ingredients, making them a handy standby in your recipe repertoire.

2 x 180g tins of tuna, drained (Shines if possible)

1 bunch of spring onions, very thinly sliced

200g coarse fresh white breadcrumbs

300g light mayonnaise

150g mature Cheddar cheese, grated

150g frozen sweetcorn

1 egg yolk

3 tbsp rapeseed oil

TO SERVE

4 brioche burger buns, split

soft lettuce leaves

2 ripe tomatoes, sliced

sea salt and freshly ground black pepper

Place the tuna in a bowl with two-thirds of the spring onions and half of the breadcrumbs, 200g of the mayonnaise and half of the Cheddar. Fold in the frozen sweetcorn and the egg yolk and season generously, then mix well to combine. Shape into 4 x 10cm patties.

Put the rest of the breadcrumbs in a shallow dish and season generously. Whisk the remaining 100g of mayonnaise with 4 teaspoons of water in a shallow bowl and use this to coat the tuna patties, then gently coat them in the seasoned breadcrumbs. Keep extra portions in the fridge or freeze at this stage.

Preheat the grill to medium.

Heat 2 tablespoons of the oil in a large non-stick frying pan over a medium heat. Add the tuna burgers and cook for 4–5 minutes, until crisp and golden brown. Add the remaining tablespoon of oil to the pan, turn the burgers over and cook for another 4–5 minutes.

Meanwhile, lightly toast the burger buns under the grill or on a hot griddle pan. Tip the remaining spring onions into a small bowl and stir in the remaining cheese. Add a dollop on top of each burger and pop under the grill for 1–2 minutes, until bubbling.

To serve, put the burger bun bottoms on plates and add the lettuce and one or two tomato slices. Top each one with a tuna melt burger, then add the burger bun tops.

30 MINS

 20 MINS

 LOADS OF VEG

Honey and Soy Glazed Salmon with Green Quinoa Serves 4

100ml soy sauce

3 tbsp honey

a good pinch of chilli flakes

1 tbsp rapeseed oil

1 tsp sesame oil

4 x 125g salmon fillets, skin on (scaled)

FOR THE QUINOA

150g quinoa

300ml vegetable stock

100g curly kale

100g baby spinach leaves

100g shelled pistachios, toasted and chopped

75g watercress

1 red onion, finely chopped

1 avocado, halved, stoned and diced

½ cucumber, deseeded and finely chopped

2 tbsp chopped fresh coriander

sea salt and freshly ground black pepper

TO GARNISH

lime wedges

This glaze is a staple in our house and can be used on cooked salmon fillets, pork or chicken. Simply pop them into a heated frying pan with a little oil, then pour over some of the glaze and spoon it over as the mixture thickens and becomes syrupy. Trout fillets are also a good alternative to salmon and are often good value for money.

Rinse the quinoa and put in a pan with the stock. Bring to the boil, then cover with a lid and reduce the heat to low. Simmer for 10–12 minutes, until all the liquid has been absorbed and the quinoa is just tender. Place in a bowl. This can be kept in the fridge at this stage.

Put the soy sauce, honey and chilli flakes into a small bowl or use a jar if you plan to keep it. Whisk or shake until combined.

Take the quinoa out of the fridge 20 minutes before serving to bring it up to room temperature. Meanwhile, prep the rest of the ingredients and fold them into the quinoa, then season to taste.

When you're ready to cook the salmon, season the fillets. Heat a non-stick frying pan over a medium heat. Add the rapeseed and sesame oil, swirling them around to combine. Fry the salmon fillets, skin side up, for 2–3 minutes, until lightly golden. Turn them over and cook for another 4 minutes. Increase the heat to high and pour in the honey and soy mixture. Allow to simmer for a couple of minutes, spooning the sauce over the fillets as it thickens to a syrupy glaze.

To serve, put the green quinoa on a serving platter and sit the salmon fillets on top. Drizzle over the syrupy sauce and garnish with lime wedges.

15 MINS

 1 HR

 LOADS OF VEG

FREEZER FRIENDLY (SAUCE)

2 red onions, roughly chopped

2 red peppers, roughly chopped

2 yellow peppers, roughly chopped

4 garlic cloves, peeled

2 tbsp rapeseed oil

1 x 400g tin of plum tomatoes (see the intro)

1 tbsp balsamic vinegar

400g orzo

400ml vegetable stock

sea salt and freshly ground black pepper

TO SERVE

a small handful of fresh basil leaves

freshly grated Parmesan cheese

Orzo with Roasted Vegetable Sauce Serves 4-6

This is a lovely quick recipe that's light on prep for busy nights. If you want to make it vegan, use vegetable stock and leave out the Parmesan. Look for DOP San Marzano canned whole peeled plum tomatoes, which are a little more expensive than the regular ones but are worth every cent. They've got the most fantastic flavour and will elevate this dish into something special.

Preheat the oven to 180°C (350°F/gas mark 4).

Put the onions, peppers and garlic in a roasting tin and drizzle over the oil. Season generously and roast for 20 minutes.

Drain the tomatoes, reserving the juice. Add the tomatoes to the roasting vegetables and drizzle over the balsamic vinegar. Give everything a good stir and roast for another 20 minutes, until the vegetables are nicely charred but not burned.

Transfer the vegetable mixture to a pan with the reserved tomato juice and blitz with a hand-held blender until smooth. This can be made in advance or frozen at this stage.

Stir the orzo into the roasted vegetable sauce and simmer gently on the hob for about 10 minutes, stirring often so that the orzo doesn't stick to the bottom of the pan, until the sauce has thickened and reduced and the orzo is starting to soften. Add the stock, a little at a time, until the orzo is tender but still with a little bite, with a risotto-like texture.

To serve, divide between bowls and scatter over the basil and some Parmesan.

15 MINS

 1 HR

 LOADS OF VEG

 FREEZER FRIENDLY

2 tbsp rapeseed oil

2 large onions, finely chopped

4 garlic cloves, crushed

5cm piece of fresh root ginger, peeled and finely grated

2 tbsp cumin seeds

2 tbsp medium curry powder

2 tsp ground coriander

2 tsp ground turmeric

1 tsp hot chilli powder

1kg sweet potatoes, peeled and cut into 1.5cm chunks

250g red lentils

2 x 400g tins of chopped tomatoes

2 x 400ml tins of coconut milk

600ml vegetable stock

20g fresh coriander, chopped

2 tsp nigella seeds (optional)

sea salt and freshly ground black pepper

TO SERVE

warm naan (optional)

Sweet Potato, Lentil and Coconut Curry Serves 6-8

This is a great curry to make if you want extra portions for another day – you may just need to add a good splash of water if the curry has thickened too much once it has chilled down. Alternatively, use the chilled curry as a filling for curried sweet potato pastries using ready-made puff pastry.

Heat the oil in a casserole over a medium to high heat and sauté the onions for 6–8 minutes, until softened and just beginning to brown around the edges. Stir in the garlic and ginger and cook for another minute.

Sprinkle over the spices, then tip in the sweet potatoes and toss until evenly combined. Add the lentils, tomatoes, coconut milk and stock. Season generously, then reduce the heat and simmer gently, uncovered, for about 30 minutes, stirring occasionally, until the sweet potatoes and lentils are cooked through but still holding their shape. Keep extra portions in the fridge or freeze at this stage.

To serve, ladle the curry into bowls and scatter over the coriander and nigella seeds (if using). Have some warm naan alongside to mop it all up if liked.

30 MINS

 1½ HRS

 LOADS OF VEG

 FREEZER FRIENDLY

2 tbsp rapeseed oil

2 red onions, finely chopped

2 celery sticks, finely chopped

3 mixed peppers, cut into bite-sized pieces

4 garlic cloves, crushed

1 tbsp ground cumin

2 tsp smoked paprika

2 tsp chipotle paste or chilli powder

2 tsp ground cinnamon

1 tsp dried oregano

1 small pumpkin, peeled, seeded and cut into 2cm chunks (or see the intro)

2 x 400g tins of chopped tomatoes

2 tbsp tomato purée

500ml vegetable stock

2 x 400g tins of black beans, drained and rinsed

1 x 400g tin of red kidney beans, drained and rinsed

25g dark chocolate (at least 70% cocoa solids), finely chopped

1 tbsp light muscovado sugar

sea salt and freshly ground black pepper

Vegetarian Chilli
Serves 6-8

TO SERVE

2 limes, cut into wedges

1 bunch of spring onions, thinly sliced

2 ripe avocados, halved, peeled, stoned and sliced

20g fresh coriander, leaves picked and roughly chopped

18–24 small flour tortillas

This tastes even better when reheated. I like to serve it with coriander, spring onions, avocado, lime wedges and tortillas, but grated cheese and soured cream are also delicious. Try butternut squash or a couple of sweet potatoes instead of the pumpkin depending on what's available.

Heat the oil in a casserole with a lid over a medium to high heat. Sauté the onions, celery and peppers with a pinch of salt for 8–10 minutes, until softened and starting to caramelise around the edges. Stir in the garlic, spices and oregano and sauté for another 2 minutes, until fragrant.

Stir in the pumpkin, tinned tomatoes and tomato purée along with the stock. Bring to the boil, then reduce the heat and cover. Simmer gently for 45 minutes, then tip in the black beans and kidney beans. Give everything a good stir and season generously. Cook, uncovered, for another 30 minutes, until all the vegetables are tender and the sauce has nicely thickened. Add the chocolate and sugar, stirring until melted. Keep extra portions in the fridge or freeze at this stage.

To serve, put the warm chilli in a serving bowl with separate bowls of lime wedges, spring onions, avocado slices and coriander. Have the warm tortillas to hand and allow everyone to help themselves.

15 MINS

 1 HR 30 MINS

 LOADS OF VEG

 FREEZER FRIENDLY

2 tbsp nigella seeds, plus extra to garnish

2 tbsp cumin seeds

2 tbsp coriander seeds, coarsely ground

3 tbsp rapeseed oil

2 large onions, finely chopped

2 tsp ground turmeric

200g dried yellow split peas, rinsed

2 x 400ml tins of coconut milk

1.2 litres vegetable stock

2 large butternut squash

300g baby spinach leaves

juice of 1 lemon

a good handful of fresh coriander leaves

sea salt and freshly ground black pepper

TO GARNISH

coconut yoghurt

Spinach and Spilt Pea Dahl
Serves 4-6

A great recipe to make in a large batch so that you can freeze it in portions. Nigella seeds are tiny black seeds that are big on flavour. If you can't find them in the supermarket, you'll easily pick them up in a health food store. They were mentioned in the Bible's Old Testament and found in Tutankhamun's tomb, making them one of the oldest spices known to have been used.

Add 4 teaspoons each of the nigella, cumin and coriander seeds to a casserole over a medium heat and toast for 1 minute, until aromatic. Add half of the oil with the onion and a pinch of salt and sauté for about 5 minutes, until softened. Stir in the turmeric and then the split peas and cook for another minute. Add the coconut milk and stock and bring to a simmer. Cover and simmer gently for about 1 hour 20 minutes, stirring occasionally, until the split peas are tender and starting to break down. Keep extra portions in the fridge or freeze at this stage.

Meanwhile, preheat the oven to 180°C (350°F/gas mark 4).

Peel the butternut squash, then cut it in half and remove the seeds. Cut into 1.5cm chunks and put in a roasting tin (or keep in an airtight container in the fridge for up to three days if you want to get ahead). Toss with the rest of the oil and the remaining 2 teaspoons each of nigella, cumin and coriander seeds. Season generously and roast for 25–30 minutes, until tender and starting to caramelise around the edges, giving it all a gentle stir halfway through cooking.

When the split peas are tender, give the dahl a good stir so that some of the peas break down to thicken it up but some are still holding their shape. Stir in the spinach, then cover the casserole again and let it just wilt. Add the lemon juice and season to taste.

To serve, spoon the dahl into bowls and scatter over the roasted butternut squash and coriander leaves, then garnish each one with a pinch of nigella seeds and a dollop of coconut yoghurt.

CHAPTER 3 HOME COMFORTS

20 MINS

 30 MINS

 FREEZER FRIENDLY

2 large chicken fillets

75g plain flour

2 eggs

2 tbsp milk

150g fresh white breadcrumbs

30g freshly grated Parmesan cheese, plus extra to garnish

300g spaghetti

4 tbsp rapeseed oil

1 x 120g ball of buffalo mozzarella, cut into 4 slices

a small handful of fresh basil leaves

FOR THE SAUCE

1 tbsp rapeseed oil

1 small onion, finely chopped

1 garlic clove, thinly sliced

1 x 400g tin of chopped tomatoes

1 tbsp red wine vinegar

½ tsp fresh thyme leaves

a good pinch of caster sugar

sea salt and freshly ground black pepper

TO SERVE

mixed leaf salad

Chicken Parmigiana
Serves 4

An ideal meal for a busy weeknight as the chicken and sauce are both perfect for freezing. Cook the chicken from frozen and just give it an extra few minutes under the grill.

First make the sauce. Heat the oil in a sauté pan over a medium heat. Sauté the onion and garlic for 3–4 minutes, until softened but not coloured. Season, then add the tomatoes, vinegar, thyme and sugar. Bring to a simmer and cook for 5 minutes, stirring. Blitz with a hand-held blender until smooth. This can be made in advance or frozen.

Meanwhile, place the chicken on a chopping board and cut each fillet in half lengthways. Spread them out and cover with parchment paper, then bash with a rolling pin until they are about 1cm thick.

Put the flour in a dish and season generously. Put the eggs in a separate dish with the milk and season, then beat lightly with a fork. Put the breadcrumbs and Parmesan into a third dish, stirring to combine. Dust each chicken escalope in the seasoned flour, then dip into the beaten eggs and finally coat it in the breadcrumbs. Arrange on a plate. At this stage, these can be covered with cling film and kept in the fridge or freeze them stacked between sheets of parchment paper.

Cook the spaghetti in a pan of boiling salted water for 10–12 minutes (or according to the packet instructions) until just tender (al dente).

Meanwhile, preheat the grill to high.

Heat the oil in a large non-stick frying pan over a medium heat. Cook the escalopes for 2–3 minutes on each side, until crisp and golden. Put on a baking tray. Spoon a little of the sauce on each one and top with a piece of mozzarella. Flash under the grill for 2–3 minutes, until the mozzarella is bubbling.

Drain the spaghetti, reserving a mugful of the cooking water, and toss it in the rest of the tomato sauce. Add some of the cooking water, if needed to loosen the sauce, then transfer to a serving bowl and garnish with the basil leaves and a little grated Parmesan.

Serve the baking tray straight to the table with the bowl of spaghetti and a bowl of salad so everyone can help themselves.

15 MINS

 15 MINS

Spiced Chicken BLT Burgers
Makes 4

2 tbsp Dunnes Stores Simply Better Organic Spicy Pepper and Herb Seasoning

2 large chicken fillets

2 tbsp rapeseed oil

4 rindless smoked streaky bacon rashers (dry-cured if possible)

2 small ripe avocados

4 sourdough burger buns

2 tbsp mayonnaise

2 tsp Dijon mustard

2 tsp tomato ketchup

50g baby spinach leaves

2 plum tomatoes, thinly sliced

1 small red onion, thinly sliced

sea salt and freshly ground black pepper

TO SERVE

thick-cut crisps (optional)

Do you struggle to find recipes that take very little time but the whole family will love? Look no further than these fully loaded chicken burgers. I've used some spicy pepper and herb seasoning from the Simply Better range in Dunnes Stores, but feel free to swap with whatever spice blend you have.

Preheat the grill to high.

Put the spicy pepper and herb seasoning in a shallow dish and season generously. Put the chicken on a chopping board and cut each fillet in half so that you have four thin fillets, then drizzle over half of the oil and toss to coat in the spice mixture. Heat the remaining oil in a large non-stick frying pan and cook the chicken for 5–6 minutes, turning once. Stack them up on one side of the pan and fry the bacon for a few minutes, until cooked and tender. Snip each rasher into three pieces.

While the chicken is cooking, stone, peel and slice the avocados and toast the cut sides of the buns under the grill. Spread the buns with mayonnaise, then add a smear of mustard to the bottoms and ketchup to the tops. Top with a handful of spinach and a few tomato slices, then arrange the chicken on top with the bacon, avocado and red onion. Press down lightly and arrange on plates with a small handful of crisps, if liked, to serve.

20 MINS + MARINATING

 30 MINS

 FREEZER FRIENDLY

100ml milk kefir

4 small chicken fillets

100g plain flour

75g panko breadcrumbs

3 tbsp freshly grated Parmesan cheese

1 large egg

75ml vegetable oil

FOR THE POTATO SALAD

500g waxy baby new potatoes (such as Charlotte, Anya or Jersey Royals)

2 tbsp olive or rapeseed oil

1 tbsp white wine vinegar

1 tsp Dijon mustard

1 small red onion, very finely chopped

3 tbsp milk kefir

2 tbsp mayonnaise

2 tsp horseradish sauce

200g baby cucumbers, sliced

2 tbsp chopped fresh dill, plus extra to garnish

sea salt and freshly ground black pepper

TO SERVE

lemon wedges

Chicken Schnitzel with Kefir Potato Salad Serves 4

Kefir is a fantastic superfood that is so good for your gut health that I try to get it into our diet any way I can. It's a live fermented food that is packed full of beneficial bacteria and yeasts. Try to track down Always Organic by Blakes, which is made in the Food Hub in Drumshanbo, Co. Leitrim, from locally soured organic milk.

To marinate the chicken, put the kefir in a shallow dish and add a good pinch of salt and plenty of pepper. Place a layer of cling film on the work surface and put the chicken fillets on top. Cover with another piece of cling film and using a rolling pin, bash each one until it's 3mm thick all over. Put into the kefir and cover with cling film. Chill for at least 2 hours to tenderise or overnight is ideal.

To make the potato salad, tip the potatoes into a large pan of salted water. Bring to the boil, then reduce the heat and simmer for 15 minutes, until tender.

Meanwhile, whisk the oil, vinegar, mustard and red onion together in a large bowl and season generously. Drain the potatoes and halve or quarter them, then toss in the mustard dressing to coat.

Mix the kefir with the mayonnaise and horseradish in a bowl to make a thin dressing. When the potatoes are cool, gently fold in the cucumbers and dill and toss everything in the kefir dressing.

Put the flour on a plate and season. Mix the breadcrumbs and Parmesan in a dish. Drain the chicken fillets from the kefir, shaking off any excess, and whisk in the egg. Dust each drained chicken fillet in the flour, then dip it into the egg and coat in the crumbs. Put on a plate. These can be covered with cling film and kept in the fridge or freeze them stacked between sheets of parchment paper.

Heat the oil in a large frying pan over a medium to high heat and cook the chicken schnitzels two at a time. Fry for 2–3 minutes on each side, until cooked through and golden, then lift out onto kitchen paper to drain. Keep them warm in a low oven while you cook the rest.

Arrange the chicken schnitzels on plates with the potato salad and garnish with a little extra dill and lemon wedges to serve.

10 MINS

 30 MINS

One-Pot Pasta with Bacon and Petit Pois Serves 4

1 tbsp rapeseed oil

200g rindless streaky bacon rashers, chopped

1 large onion, very finely chopped

4 garlic cloves, crushed

600ml chicken stock

350ml milk

250g spaghetti

250g frozen petit pois

4 tbsp freshly grated Parmesan cheese, plus extra shavings to garnish

sea salt and freshly ground black pepper

This is a clever one-pot pasta that is packed with flavour with just one pan for washing up! It's the kind of dish you can properly cobble together when the cupboards are looking bare.

Heat the oil in a sauté pan over a high heat. Add the bacon and cook for 2–3 minutes, until crisp and golden. Transfer the bacon to a plate using a slotted spoon, leaving the fat the bacon has released in the pan.

Reduce the heat to medium and sauté the onion and garlic for 3–4 minutes, until softened but not coloured.

Pour in the stock, scraping the bottom of the pan to remove any sediment. Stir in the milk, then season with salt and pepper and bring to the boil over a high heat. Add the spaghetti and simmer vigorously for about 12 minutes, until the pasta is just tender but still with a little bite (al dente) and the liquid has reduced enough to form a silky glaze. Stir in the petit pois about 3 minutes before the end of the cooking time so that they can also cook through.

Just before serving, fold in the Parmesan with most of the crispy bacon. Divide between bowls and scatter over the rest of the bacon with some Parmesan shavings to serve.

30 MINS

 45 MINS

 FREEZER FRIENDLY

Sausage-Stuffed Conchiglioni
Serves 4

1 tbsp rapeseed oil

1 red onion, finely chopped

6 Jane Russell toasted fennel and chilli sausages

a small handful of fresh sage leaves, roughly chopped

2 x 280g jars of tomato and mascarpone sauce (or similar)

350g conchiglioni (large pasta shells)

150g Gorgonzola or buffalo mozzarella, cut into cubes

4 tbsp freshly grated Parmesan cheese

sea salt and freshly ground black pepper

TO SERVE

sautéed spinach and garlic (optional)

TO GARNISH

crispy sage leaves (optional)

Conchiglioni or large pasta shells can now be found in lots of supermarkets, but if you can't get hold of them, simply use the smaller variety, conchiglie, and toss all the ingredients together before baking. Of course, you can use any type of premium sausage, but Jane Russell's meaty toasted fennel and chilli ones are so tasty they're hard to beat!

Preheat the oven to 180°C (350°F/gas mark 4).

Heat the oil in a large non-stick frying pan over a medium to high heat. Sauté the onion for 3–4 minutes, until softened and just beginning to catch around the edges.

Meanwhile, remove the sausages from their skins and divide into small balls. Add to the onion with the sage and sauté for another 2–3 minutes, until browned. Add 5–6 tablespoons of the tomato and mascarpone sauce to moisten the mixture a little and season to taste.

Put the pasta shells into a large pan of boiling salted water and return to the boil. Simmer for 3 minutes, then drain.

Pour the rest of the opened jar of tomato and mascarpone sauce into a shallow baking dish about 1.5 litres in capacity. Arrange the pasta shells on top and fill with the sausage mixture. Pour over the other jar of tomato and mascarpone sauce and scatter the Gorgonzola or mozzarella and the Parmesan on top. This can be covered with cling film and kept in the fridge or is perfect for freezing.

Bake for 20–25 minutes, until bubbling and golden, then crumble over the crispy sage leaves (if using).

Serve straight to the table with a bowl of sautéed spinach and garlic if liked.

20 MINS

 30 MINS

Mango-Glazed Gammon and Pineapple Serves 4

6 tbsp spiced mango chutney

2 tbsp lemon juice

4 x 200g dry-cured gammon steaks

8 ready-prepared fresh pineapple rings

FOR THE COLCANNON

675g potatoes, peeled and cut into small pieces

300g green cabbage or spring greens, roughly chopped (any tough stalks removed)

120ml milk

1 bunch of spring onions, thinly sliced

25g butter

sea salt and freshly ground black pepper

A twist on an old favourite that I've served with some creamy colcannon – the combination works very well.

Put the potatoes in a pan of boiling salted water and return to the boil, then reduce the heat and simmer for 12 minutes, until almost tender.

Meanwhile, preheat the grill to high.

Put the mango chutney in a small bowl with the lemon juice, stirring to combine. Arrange the gammon steaks and pineapple on a baking tray lined with foil. Grill for 6 minutes, turning once.

Turn everything in the baking tin over again and brush with most of the glaze. Grill for another 3–4 minutes, until the gammon steaks are cooked through and the pineapple looks sticky and golden. Leave to rest for a few minutes while you finish the colcannon.

Add the cabbage or spring greens to the potatoes and cook for another 3 minutes, until the potatoes are tender and the greens are nicely wilted. Drain into a colander in the sink. Pour the milk into the same pan and tip in the spring onions. Bring to a quick simmer, then return the potatoes and greens to the pan along with the butter and crush to make a rough mash. Season with salt and pepper.

Arrange the gammon steaks on plates with the pineapple rings and the colcannon. Any leftover glaze can be put into a small dish for dipping.

30 MINS

 3 HRS

❋ FREEZER FRIENDLY

Sticky Ginger Ham, Egg and Chips Serves 4-6

2 unsmoked ham hocks (each about 1.5kg)

3 star anise

10 black peppercorns

2 bay leaves

1 orange, cut into slices

675g potatoes, unpeeled and cut into chunky chips

4 tbsp rapeseed oil

75g dark muscovado sugar

3 tbsp Dijon mustard

½ tsp ground allspice

3 knobs of stem ginger, finely chopped, plus 1 tbsp syrup from the jar

4–6 large eggs

sea salt and freshly ground black pepper

TO SERVE

tomato ketchup

Ham hocks are very affordable and give a great ratio of meat. If you have the time, cook them at the weekend to use during the week.

Put the hams hocks in a large pan with the star anise, peppercorns, bay leaves and orange slices, then pour over enough water to cover. Bring to a simmer, then reduce the heat and cover partially with a lid. Simmer very gently for 1½ hours, topping up the water if necessary, until the ham hocks are tender but not falling off the bone. Transfer to a chopping board and leave until cool enough to handle.

Preheat the oven to 180°C (350°F/gas mark 4).

When the hocks have cooled a little, use a sharp knife to cut away the skin, leaving a layer of fat. Put in a baking tray lined with tin foil and bake for 20–25 minutes, until the fat starts to crisp up.

Meanwhile, put the potatoes in a pan of boiling salted water and bring back to the boil. Reduce the heat and simmer for 5 minutes, until softened slightly, then drain and leave to steam dry for a few minutes.

Pour 3 tablespoons of the oil into a large baking tin and heat for 5 minutes. Meanwhile, toss the chips with salt, then carefully tip them into the hot oil and roast for about 30 minutes, turning halfway through cooking, until crisp and golden.

Mix the sugar, mustard, allspice, stem ginger and syrup in a small bowl. Brush half over the ham hocks and return to the oven for another 20–25 minutes, brushing with more glaze every 10 minutes, until the ham hocks have a sticky crust and the meat is meltingly tender. Leave to rest for 10 minutes, then carve into chunks. This can be covered with cling film and chilled or is perfect for freezing.

About 5 minutes before the chips are ready and while the ham hocks are resting, heat a large non-stick frying pan over a medium to high heat. Add the rest of the oil, then break in the eggs, season with salt and fry to your liking.

Arrange slices of the sticky ginger ham on plates with the egg and chips with some tomato ketchup alongside to serve.

30 MINS

 1 HR

❋ FREEZER FRIENDLY

1 tbsp rapeseed oil

8 premium pork sausages

2 large onions, thinly sliced

1 tsp fresh thyme leaves

2 tbsp sherry or red wine vinegar

2 tbsp plain flour

500ml beef stock

1 tbsp redcurrant jelly

FOR THE CHAMP

675g potatoes, peeled and cut into large chunks

1 bunch of spring onions, thinly sliced

100ml milk

25g butter

1 tbsp Dijon mustard

sea salt and freshly ground black pepper

TO SERVE

buttered cabbage (optional)

Sausage and Champ Pie
Serves 4

A comforting take on sausage and mash. You can freeze this pie for busy weeknights and if you want to cook it straight from frozen, just give it an extra 10–15 minutes in the oven.

To make the champ, tip the potatoes into a large pan and cover with cold water. Add a pinch of salt and bring to the boil, then reduce the heat and simmer for 20 minutes, until tender.

Meanwhile, preheat the oven to 200°C (400°F/gas mark 6).

Heat the oil in a sauté pan and cook the sausages for 6–8 minutes, until browned. Transfer to a plate. Add the onions and thyme and sauté for 8–10 minutes, until well softened and lightly browned. Pour in the vinegar and allow to bubble down, then sprinkle over the flour. Cook for 1 minute, stirring, then gradually add the stock and stir in the redcurrant jelly. Season with salt and pepper and cook for 5–6 minutes, until you have a thick, glossy gravy. Cut the sausages into thick slices.

When the potatoes are cooked, drain and return them to the pan, then allow to steam dry for another few minutes, shaking the pan occasionally to prevent them sticking. Put the spring onions and milk in a small pan and gently heat (or do this in the microwave). Mash the potatoes until smooth, then beat in the butter and mustard. Pour in the milk mixture and beat again until smooth.

Scatter the sausages on the bottom of a 1.5-litre baking dish, then spoon over the onion gravy. Cover with dollops of the champ and spread it out evenly to cover the sausage mixture completely. Bake for 20–25 minutes, until golden brown and bubbling. This can be covered with cling film before baking and kept in the fridge or is perfect for freezing.

Serve straight to the table with a bowl of buttered cabbage if liked.

15 MINS

 15 MINS

Ultimate Pasta Carbonara
Serves 4

350g spaghetti

1 tbsp olive or rapeseed oil

2 garlic cloves, peeled

100g pancetta cubes

3 eggs

1 egg yolk

75g freshly grated Parmesan cheese, plus extra to garnish

25g freshly grated Pecorino Romano cheese

a pinch of grated nutmeg (optional)

sea salt and freshly ground black pepper

One of the simplest pasta dishes, but the devil is in the details to get that perfect consistency – I've added an additional egg yolk for extra richness. It also uses a mixture of Parmesan and Pecorino Romano, a hard, salty ewe's milk cheese popular in central Italy. It has a lighter flavour than Parmesan and the combination seems to have the perfect balance.

Add a good pinch of salt to a large pan of water and bring to a rolling boil. Swirl in the spaghetti and simmer for 10–12 minutes, until just tender but still with a little bite (al dente).

Meanwhile, heat the oil in a large non-stick frying pan over a medium heat. Squash the garlic cloves with the blade of a knife to bruise them and add to the pan with the pancetta. Sauté for about 5 minutes, until the pancetta is crisp and golden. The garlic has now imparted its flavour, so take it out with a slotted spoon and discard.

Break the eggs into a bowl and add the yolk, then lightly beat with a fork to combine. Stir in the Parmesan and Pecorino and season generously with pepper.

When the pasta is cooked, scoop out a small cupful of the pasta cooking water, then drain the pasta well. Tip it into the frying pan and toss to coat in the pancetta mixture, then quickly tip in the egg mixture. Using a tongs, toss the pasta quickly. Once it has begun to thicken, add a splash of the reserved cooking water to loosen to a sauce consistency.

Using a long-pronged fork, twist the pasta into warmed bowls and add a pinch of nutmeg, if liked. Scatter with a little extra Parmesan to serve.

15 MINS

 1¼ HRS

 FREEZER FRIENDLY

Lamb Ragù with Pappardelle
Serves 4

2 tbsp rapeseed oil

1 onion, finely chopped

1 celery stick, finely chopped

1 carrot, finely chopped

2 garlic cloves, crushed

½ tsp chilli flakes

100ml white wine

2 tbsp tomato purée

400g minced lamb

2 tsp dried harissa spice seasoning

½ tsp ground cinnamon

1 x 400g tin of chopped tomatoes

1 roasted red pepper (from a tin or jar), drained and finely diced

300ml chicken stock

1 bay leaf

225g dried egg pappardelle

a small handful of fresh mint leaves or flat-leaf parsley

sea salt and freshly ground black pepper

This ragù is wonderfully rich and sweet and only improves with time, making it a great one to double up, ready for a rainy day – or a hectic one. Layer it up with chargrilled aubergines and finish it with a béchamel sauce and you've got a moussaka.

Heat a heavy-based casserole over a medium to high heat. Add the oil and swirl it around, then tip in the onion, celery and carrot and sauté for about 5 minutes, until the vegetables start to brown slightly. Season with salt and pepper, stir in the garlic and chilli flakes and sauté for 30 seconds.

Pour in the wine and allow to bubble down, then stir in the tomato purée. Tip in the minced lamb and sauté until lightly browned. Stir in the harissa and cinnamon, then add the tomatoes, red pepper and stock, stirring to combine. Add the bay leaf and bring to the boil, then reduce the heat to a simmer and cover. Cook for 30 minutes, stirring occasionally.

Remove the lid and cook for another 25–30 minutes, stirring occasionally, until all the excess liquid has reduced and the ragù is nice and thick. This can be covered with cling film and kept in the fridge or is perfect for freezing.

About 15 minutes before you're ready to serve, bring a large pan of salted water to a rolling boil. Tip in the pappardelle and cook for 5–6 minutes, until tender but still with a little bite (al dente). Drain in a colander and tip onto a serving platter.

Spoon the lamb ragù over the pappardelle, then tear up the mint or parsley and scatter on top. Serve family-style at the table.

20 MINS

 30 MINS

 LOADS OF VEG

 FREEZER FRIENDLY

1 garlic clove, crushed

1 tbsp chopped fresh rosemary

8 lamb cutlets, well-trimmed

1 tbsp rapeseed oil

200ml dry cider or white wine

1 tbsp redcurrant jelly

a squeeze of lemon juice

FOR THE CELERIAC CRUSH

250g potatoes, peeled and cut into chunks

250g celeriac, peeled and cut into chunks

200g pointed green cabbage, shredded (tough stalks removed)

1 garlic clove, crushed

4 tbsp milk

a knob of butter

sea salt and freshly ground black pepper

TO SERVE

buttered carrots

Rosemary Lamb Cutlets with Celeriac Crush Serves 4

The celeriac crush is the perfect accompaniment for these sticky lamb cutlets. Celeriac is an underused vegetable that is high in fibre and packed full of goodness. Ask your butcher to French trim the lamb cutlets or you can find them in some supermarkets.

Put the potatoes and celeriac in a pan of boiling salted water and simmer for 15 minutes, until almost tender.

Meanwhile, mix the garlic with half of the rosemary and season with salt and pepper. Smear the lamb cutlets all over with the oil, then press on the garlic mixture.

Heat a large non-stick frying pan over a medium heat and cook the lamb cutlets for 6–8 minutes, turning once, until just cooked through and tender. Transfer to a plate and keep warm.

Pour the cider or wine into the pan and allow to bubble down. Using a wooden spoon, stir in the redcurrant jelly and lemon juice with the rest of the rosemary. Bring to a simmer and reduce for 8–10 minutes, until slightly syrupy.

Stir the cabbage into the potatoes and celeriac and simmer for another 2 minutes, until all the vegetables are tender, then drain in the sink. Add the garlic and milk to the same pan, then tip the vegetables back in and roughly crush with the butter. Season to taste.

Return the rested lamb chops to the frying pan and turn them in the sauce to glaze. Arrange on plates with the celeriac crush and some buttered carrots to serve.

20 MINS + MARINATING

 20 MINS

 LOADS OF VEG

 FREEZER FRIENDLY

100g Greek yoghurt

3 garlic cloves, minced

2 tbsp rapeseed oil, plus extra for brushing

2 tbsp red wine vinegar

2 tsp freshly grated root ginger

1 tbsp tandoori spice mix

400g lean lamb leg steaks, cut into bite-sized pieces

1 red onion, cut into chunks

1 yellow pepper, cut into chunks

1 orange pepper, cut into chunks

fresh coriander leaves

sea salt and freshly ground black pepper

TO SERVE

warm naan

tomato and red onion salad

raita

Tandoori-Spiced Lamb and Vegetable Skewers Serves 4

For something spicy that has plenty of flavour, try these succulent lamb skewers steeped in tandoori spices. The longer you can marinate them, the better they will taste. If the weather is fine, pop them on the barbecue – that way, your hob stays nice and clean. A win-win in my book!

Put the yoghurt in a large bowl with the garlic, oil, vinegar and ginger. Stir in the tandoori spice and season generously, then stir in the lamb until evenly combined. Cover with cling film and set aside to marinate for 30 minutes at room temperature or up to three days in the fridge is good. This is also perfect for freezing.

Preheat the grill or a griddle pan to high.

Thread the marinated lamb, red onion chunks and peppers onto 20cm metal or bamboo skewers (if using bamboo skewers, soak them in cold water first). Arrange on a plate and brush the vegetables with a little more oil.

Place on the grill or pan and cook for 5 minutes, then turn and cook for another 5 minutes, until the lamb is tender and the vegetables are slightly charred. Transfer to a serving platter and scatter over a few fresh coriander leaves.

Serve family-style with warm naan, tomato and red onion salad and raita.

15 MINS

 1 HR

 FREEZER FRIENDLY

Chipotle Beef Crunchy Tacos
Serves 4-6

This clever recipe uses a ready-made smoky chipotle sauce and results in an intense, complex flavour. As it's a midweek meal, I'm making full use of the ready-made accompaniments that are now in all the shops, but of course you can make your own if you prefer and if time is on your side.

25g beef dripping

500g minced beef steak

2 large onions, thinly sliced

4 garlic cloves, finely chopped

250ml chipotle marinade (Irish made if possible)

500ml beef stock

1 shot of espresso (optional)

1 x 400g tin of black beans

1 x 170g packet of hard shell tacos

sea salt and freshly ground black pepper

TO SERVE

shredded white cabbage

ready-made soured cream and chive dip

guacamole

tomato salsa

fresh coriander leaves

Heat a casserole over a high heat. Tip in the beef dripping and swirl it around to heat it up. Add the mince and sauté quickly until browned. Add the onions and garlic and continue to sauté for another 10 minutes, until the onions are well softened and beginning to caramelise.

Stir in the chipotle marinade and cook for 2–3 minutes, until sticky. Pour in the stock and espresso (if using). Drain the black beans and add the juices from the tin, stirring to combine. Season generously with pepper and simmer vigorously for 20 minutes. Stir in the black beans and simmer for another 10 minutes, until the beef is tender and the liquid has completely reduced. This can be covered with cling film and kept in the fridge or is perfect for freezing.

Meanwhile, preheat the oven to 180°C (350°F/gas mark 4).

Place the tacos on a baking sheet and heat in the oven for 2–3 minutes.

Fill the crispy tacos with the shredded cabbage, then add a spoonful of the chipotle beef and top with the soured cream and chive dip, guacamole and tomato salsa. Scatter over the coriander to serve.

15 MINS

 1 HR

 FREEZER FRIENDLY

4 large baking potatoes
(each one 150–200g)

1 tbsp rapeseed oil

1 onion, very finely chopped

400g lean minced beef

4 tbsp tomato purée

3 tbsp dark muscovado sugar

3 tbsp apple cider vinegar

2 tbsp Dijon mustard

1 tbsp honey

2 tsp Worcestershire sauce

300ml beef stock

100g cornichons, drained – half
diced, half pared into shavings

40g butter

100g red mature Cheddar cheese,
finely grated

2 spring onions, thinly sliced

sea salt and freshly ground black
pepper

TO SERVE

chargrilled mini romaine or cos
lettuce wedges (optional)

Cheeseburger Jacket Potatoes
Serves 4

The cheeseburger spring roll has become a recent fast fusion hit,
so here are all those delicious flavours in a rich savoury mince.
Unbelievably moreish and novel enough to get the kids in your house
(no matter their age) excited.

Preheat the oven to 200°C (400°F/gas mark 6).

Prick the potatoes all over with a fork and place them directly on an
oven shelf. Bake for about 1 hour, until tender when gently squeezed.
Once cool, these can be wrapped in cling film and kept in the fridge or
frozen.

Meanwhile, heat the oil in a large non-stick frying pan over a high
heat. Add the onion and sauté for 2–3 minutes, until softened. Tip
in the beef and season generously, then quickly sauté until golden
brown, breaking up any lumps with a wooden spoon.

Add the tomato purée, sugar, vinegar, mustard, honey and
Worcestershire sauce and stir until well combined. Season to taste
and pour in the stock, then bring to a simmer and cook for another
15–20 minutes, stirring occasionally, until the sauce is nice and thick.
Fold in the diced cornichons. This can be covered with cling film and
kept in the fridge or is perfect for freezing.

Cut a cross in each baked potato and press down to reveal the flesh,
then put each one on a serving plate and lightly fluff up with a fork.
Add a knob of butter to each one, then spoon over the mince. Scatter
over the cheese and sprinkle with the spring onions. Flash back in the
oven for a couple of minutes to melt, if liked.

Scatter over the shaved cornichons and add some chargrilled romaine
or cos lettuce wedges to serve if liked.

15 MINS

 30 MINS

 LOADS OF VEG

 FREEZER FRIENDLY (BROTH)

2 garlic cloves, very thinly sliced

a 5cm piece of fresh root ginger, peeled and thinly sliced

1 lemongrass stick, trimmed to 10cm and crushed

2 x 400ml cartons of fresh beef stock

2 star anise

4 tbsp soy sauce

juice of 1 lime

2 mild fresh red chillies – 1 whole and 1 thinly sliced into rings

20g fresh coriander, leaves picked and stalks reserved

200g ramen noodles

100g shiitake mushrooms, sliced

500g baby spinach leaves

225g lean beef escalopes, sliced wafer thin

2 baby pak choi, finely sliced

100g sugar snap peas, halved

25g fresh beansprouts

1 x 40g packet of toasted nori seaweed crisps, shredded

Beef Ramen
Serves 4

Making ramen at home doesn't need to be complicated. This easy ramen recipe is ready in just 30 minutes – a quick fragrant broth with noodles and plenty of crunchy vegetables. The beef will cook on its own when stirred through the noodles and broth, but you can add it with the spinach if you prefer.

Put the garlic, ginger and lemongrass in a pan with the stock, star anise, soy sauce, lime juice, whole red chilli and coriander stalks. Bring to a simmer over a medium heat and cook for 15 minutes to allow the flavours to infuse, then strain into a clean pan. This can be covered with cling film and kept in the fridge or is perfect for freezing.

Add the ramen noodles and shiitake mushrooms to the strained broth and simmer for 2–3 minutes, until just tender. Stir in the spinach until just wilted.

To serve, divide the ramen between warmed bowls and top with the beef, pak choi, sugar snaps and beansprouts, then scatter over the coriander leaves, chilli rings and seaweed. The beef will cook immediately in the heat of the broth.

15 MINS

 1¼ HRS

 LOADS OF VEG

 FREEZER FRIENDLY

a knob of butter

350g frozen classic vegetable base mix (see the intro)

300g premium beef sausages

400g lean minced rump steak

100g fresh white breadcrumbs

4 tbsp tomato country relish (Ballymaloe or similar)

2 large eggs

2 tbsp chopped fresh flat-leaf parsley, plus extra to garnish

2 puff pastry sheets, thawed if frozen

FOR THE MASH

2 large potatoes, peeled and cut into chunks

2 carrots, peeled and cut into chunks

1 small turnip, peeled and cut into chunks

a knob of butter

4 tbsp cream or milk

sea salt and freshly ground black pepper

TO SERVE

1 x 300ml carton of ready-made beef gravy

Minced Rump Wellington
Serves 4-6

I wanted this recipe to be as easy as possible, so I've taken a shortcut by using some frozen vegetables. This mix has finely diced celery, carrot and onion, but there are all sorts of variations depending on where you shop.

Preheat the oven to 200°C (400°F/gas mark 6).

Heat a large non-stick frying pan over a high heat. Add the butter and frozen vegetables and quickly sauté for 2–3 minutes, until just tender. Season generously.

Meanwhile, remove the beef sausages from their casings and put in a large bowl with the minced steak and breadcrumbs. Add the tomato relish and one of the eggs. Tip in the vegetables and parsley, season generously and mix until evenly combined.

Unroll one of the pastry sheets onto a baking sheet lined with parchment paper. Break the remaining egg into a small bowl and beat with a pinch of salt, then brush all over the pastry. Shape the minced beef mixture into a long sausage shape on top, leaving plenty of room to make a border.

Unroll the second sheet of pastry and carefully place on top, then using a sharp knife, trim around to make a neat oblong shape. Decorate the top with any offcuts and score the edges with a fork. Brush with the rest of the beaten egg. This can be wrapped in cling film and kept in the fridge or frozen. Bake for 1 hour, until cooked through and golden brown.

Meanwhile, put the potatoes, carrots and turnip in a pan of cold salted water and bring to the boil. Reduce the heat, cover and cook for 15–20 minutes, until tender. Drain and leave to steam dry for a few minutes, then tip back into the pan and mash with the butter, cream or milk and season to taste. Keep warm until ready to serve. Once cool, this can be wrapped in cling film and kept in the fridge or frozen.

To serve, heat the gravy in a small pan or in the microwave, then pour into a gravy boat. Tip the mash into a serving bowl and scatter over a little parsley. Transfer the minced beef Wellington onto a chopping board to slice into portions at the table.

20 MINS

 30 MINS

 LOADS OF VEG

 FREEZER FRIENDLY (ROSTÏ)

1 tsp apple cider vinegar

4 large eggs

2 x 100g packets of smoked trout

100g green salad leaves

FOR THE ROOT RÖSTI

300g parsnips, peeled and coarsely grated

300g sweet potatoes, peeled and coarsely grated

3 spring onions, finely chopped

1 large egg

40g cornflour

3 tbsp rapeseed oil

sea salt and freshly ground black pepper

FOR THE DRESSING

5 tbsp crème fraîche

2 tbsp horseradish sauce

2 tbsp chopped fresh herbs (chives, dill and/or flat-leaf parsley), plus extra to garnish

TO GARNISH

lemon wedges

Smoked Trout with Root Rösti
Serves 4

I've been a lifelong fan of Mags and Ger Kirwan, who run Goatsbridge farm and are continually coming up with new products that have excellent distribution all over the country. This recipe uses their smoked trout. For real speed it's worth pulling out your food processor or try the julienne grater on a mandolin.

Put the parsnips, sweet potatoes and spring onions in a bowl. Break in the egg and sprinkle in the cornflour. Season generously and mix well to combine.

Heat half of the oil in a large non-stick frying pan over a medium heat. Add half of the root vegetable mixture in two piles and squash down with a spatula to flatten into rounds about 12cm in diameter. Cook for 4–5 minutes on each side, until cooked through and golden brown. Keep warm while you repeat the process to cook the rest. Once cool, these can be wrapped in cling film and kept in the fridge or frozen.

Meanwhile, bring a pan of water to the boil over a high heat and add the vinegar. Reduce to a gentle simmer, then use a spoon to create a whirlpool of water. Break the eggs into the edges of the pan and poach for 3½ minutes, until the whites are set and the yolks are still runny. Remove with a slotted spoon.

To make the dressing, mix together the crème fraîche, horseradish and herbs in a small bowl. Season to taste.

To serve, place a root rösti on each plate and arrange the smoked trout on top, then add a poached egg. Put some of the salad leaves alongside and drizzle over the horseradish dressing. Add a good grinding of black pepper, sprinkle over some extra herbs and garnish with a lemon wedge.

35 MINS

 20 MINS

 LOADS OF VEG

6 eggs

4 bagels

6 slices of rye bread

2 small ripe avocados

juice of ½ small lemon

225g smoked salmon strips

300g cooked black tiger prawns

1 x 200g packet of baby cucumbers, thinly sliced

3 tbsp miniature capers, drained and rinsed

avocado oil, for drizzling (optional)

2 tbsp seaweed salt

sea salt and freshly ground black pepper

FOR THE PICKLED RED ONIONS

2 small red onions, thinly sliced into rings

2 tbsp apple cider vinegar

½ tsp caster sugar

FOR THE HERBY CREAM CHEESE

150g soft cream cheese

finely grated rind and juice of ½ small lemon

20g fresh dill, fronds removed, half chopped

2 tbsp snipped fresh chives

1 tsp Dijon mustard

TO SERVE

lemon wedges (optional)

Smoked Salmon and Prawn Grazing Platter Serves 6–8

This Scandinavian-inspired sharing platter is ideal when you want to treat yourself to a special spread but haven't got much time. I love this on a warm summer evening to eat at leisure in the garden, perhaps with a cheeky glass of rosé for the night that's in it! Look for seaweed salt – Achill Island makes a lovely one harvested by the Connemara Seaweed Company.

Put the red onions in a bowl and cover with boiling water for a few minutes, then tip into a sieve to drain. Put back into the bowl with the vinegar, sugar and a good pinch of salt and stir to combine. Set aside until needed.

Put the cream cheese in a bowl with the lemon rind and juice. Add the dill, chives and mustard, season to taste and mix until well combined. This and the pickled red onions can be made in advance and kept covered in the fridge.

When ready to serve, put the eggs into a pan of boiling water and simmer for 8 minutes. Drain and cool under cold running water, then crack off the shells. Cut in half – the yolks should still be slightly soft.

Heat a griddle pan until smoking hot. Quickly char the bagels on both sides, until nicely marked, then toast the rye bread on the hot pan too.

Peel, stone and thinly slice the avocados and drizzle with the lemon juice to prevent them going brown. Arrange on a large chopping board or platter with the smoked salmon and prawns, a bowl of herby cream cheese, the pickled onions, halved eggs and baby cucumbers. Stack up the bagels and rye bread at the back end or on a separate plate. Scatter the capers over the seafood, then add a few dribbles of avocado oil (if using). Season with the seaweed salt and a grinding of black pepper, scatter over the remaining dill and garnish with lemon wedges if liked.

25 MINS

 1 HR

 FREEZER FRIENDLY

1kg potatoes, peeled and cut into chunks

250g baby spinach leaves

150g mature Cheddar cheese, grated

75g mascarpone cheese

500g skinless, boneless fish fillets (try a mixture of natural smoked cod and pollock)

300ml milk

25g butter, plus extra for greasing

1 tbsp Dijon or wholegrain mustard

2 tbsp chopped fresh flat-leaf parsley

20g fresh chives, snipped

1 egg

25g panko breadcrumbs

sea salt and freshly ground black pepper

TO SERVE

buttered peas

Giant Mornay Fishcake
Serves 4–6

An indulgent fishcake with a cheesy spinach surprise in the centre that doesn't need any chilling time before baking. It's also a great dish to prep in advance at the weekend when you've a bit more time. Use any combination of fish that your family enjoys.

Put the potatoes into a large pan of boiling salted water and cook for 15–20 minutes, until tender.

Pour a kettle of boiling water over the spinach in a colander in the sink and allow to wilt down. Set aside until cooled, then squeeze dry and put in a bowl. Fold in the Cheddar and mascarpone cheese. Season with salt and pepper.

Meanwhile, put the fish in a pan with the milk so that it's covered. Bring to a simmer, then reduce the heat and poach for 5 minutes.

Drain the potatoes and return to the pan for a few minutes to steam dry before mashing until smooth. Beat in the butter, mustard, parsley and most of the chives.

Remove the fish from the milk (discard the milk) and transfer to a plate, breaking it up into large lumps, then fold into the potato mixture and mix in the egg. Season with salt and pepper.

Preheat the oven to 180°C (350°F/gas mark 4).

Generously butter a 23cm loose-bottomed cake tin and line the base with parchment paper. Use half of the breadcrumbs to coat the dish. Add half of the fishcake mixture and push it up the sides.

Spread in the spinach mixture and add dollops of the remaining fishcake mixture to cover the filling completely. Scatter over the rest of the breadcrumbs, pressing them down gently. This can be covered in cling film and kept in the fridge or frozen.

Bake for 25 minutes, until golden brown and bubbling.

Remove from the tin, cut into wedges and scatter over the rest of the chives. Serve family-style with a bowl of buttered peas.

30 MINS

 40 MINS

 FREEZER FRIENDLY

2 x 250g cartons of ricotta cheese

2 garlic cloves, minced

2 tbsp snipped fresh chives

2 tbsp chopped fresh flat-leaf parsley

2 eggs

1 x 275g pouch of grated mozzarella

7–8 lasagne sheets (see the intro)

2 x 185g packets of poached salmon darnes, skinned and broken into chunks

250g cooked black tiger prawns

FOR THE SAUCE

50g butter, plus extra for greasing

50g plain flour

750ml milk

50g freshly grated Parmesan cheese, plus a little extra

sea salt and freshly ground black pepper

TO SERVE

sautéed fine French beans with garlic

Speedy Seafood Lasagne
Serves 6-8

This seafood spin on an Italian classic cuts out steps by using cooked salmon and prawns. Make it in batches and freeze portions to really get ahead of the game and enjoy this creamy lasagne during the week without the extra hassle. The Simply Better range at Dunnes Stores does the perfect Italian egg bronze die lasagne sheets, as they are whisper thin, but otherwise a packet of fresh lasagne sheets will also work well.

Preheat the oven to 180°C (350°F/gas mark 4).

To make the sauce, melt the butter in a small pan over a medium heat. Stir in the flour and gradually add the milk, whisking continuously. Simmer for 2–3 minutes, until thickened. Remove from the heat and season to taste, then stir in the Parmesan.

Tip the ricotta into a large bowl and add the garlic, chives, parsley, eggs and mozzarella. Season with salt and pepper and mix well to combine.

Grease a 23cm x 33cm baking dish. Spread one-quarter of the sauce over the bottom of the dish, then cover with two or three of the lasagne sheets, breaking them up to fit as necessary. Cover with one-third of the ricotta mixture and top with one-third of the seafood. Repeat the layers twice more, finishing with the sauce spread on top of a layer of lasagne sheets. Sprinkle with a little extra Parmesan.

Bake the lasagne for 30 minutes, until bubbling and golden. Leave to rest for 10 minutes, then cut into slices and arrange on plates with the sautéed French beans and garlic to serve. Once cool, portions can be covered in cling film and kept in the fridge or frozen.

20 MINS

 30 MINS

 FREEZER FRIENDLY

300g macaroni (try to find the long variety)

1 tbsp rapeseed oil

a knob of butter

2 large shallots, finely chopped

100g fennel, finely chopped

½ tsp chilli flakes

2 tbsp plain flour

1 tbsp tomato purée

½ tsp smoked paprika

450ml milk

1 tsp Worcestershire sauce

a pinch of ground nutmeg

150g mature Cheddar cheese, finely grated

50g Gruyère cheese, finely grated

1 small lemon

1 heaped tbsp chopped fresh flat-leaf parsley

1 x 250g packet of crabmeat (mixture of white and brown if possible)

sea salt and freshly ground black pepper

TO SERVE

buttered steamed samphire

Crab Mac 'n' Cheese
Serves 4

This recipe has notions! I'm playing with the flavours of a classic bisque or thermidor. There is now some very good pasteurised and vacuum-packed crabmeat in the supermarkets, so this needs just a modest amount to transform a regular mac 'n' cheese into the most luscious of dinnertime treats.

Preheat the oven to 180°C (350°F/gas mark 4).

Cook the macaroni in a large pan of boiling salted water for 7–8 minutes, until tender but still with a little bite (al dente).

Meanwhile, heat the oil in a sauté pan over a medium heat. Tip in the butter and allow to sizzle, then sauté the shallots, fennel and chilli flakes for 4–5 minutes, until softened but not coloured.

Sprinkle over the flour and cook for another minute, stirring. Stir in the tomato purée and paprika, then gradually add the milk, whisking continuously until the sauce is smooth. Simmer for 2–3 minutes, until thickened. Season with salt and pepper, then add the Worcestershire sauce and nutmeg. Remove from the heat and stir in the Cheddar and most of the Gruyère. Cut the lemon in half and squeeze in enough juice to taste, then cut the rest into small wedges.

Take a small cupful of water from the macaroni, then drain. Add the macaroni and reserved cooking water to the sauce along with the parsley, stirring until evenly combined, then fold in the crab. Divide between individual enamel baking dishes, then sprinkle over the rest of the Gruyère. Once cool, portions can be covered in cling film and kept in the fridge or frozen.

Bake for 15–20 minutes, until bubbling. Serve with the buttered samphire and lemon wedges on the side.

25 MINS + DOUGH THAWING

 25 MINS

 FREEZER FRIENDLY

1 x 500g packet of frozen sourdough balls (Golden Bake), thawed

100g honey

1 tsp chilli flakes

a little plain flour, for dusting

25g butter

2 leeks, thinly sliced

2 tbsp chopped fresh chives

1 x 290g jar of chargrilled artichokes

100g fontina cheese, grated (you could also use Gruyère, gouda or Emmental)

1 x 120g ball of buffalo mozzarella, cut into small cubes

a small handful of fresh basil leaves

25g Pecorino cheese, finely grated or pared into shavings

sea salt and freshly ground black pepper

TO SERVE

olive and wild rocket salad dressed with balsamic vinegar

Caramelised Leek and Artichoke Pizza Makes 2 large pizzas

Several supermarkets are now stocking frozen sourdough dough balls, which makes whipping up pizzas an easier task.

To defrost the dough balls, thaw them according to the packet instructions and allow them to come back to room temperature.

Pour the honey into a small pan over a low to medium heat and add the chilli flakes and 2 teaspoons of water. Bring to a simmer and cook for 30 seconds. Turn off the heat and set aside.

Preheat the oven to 200°C (400°F/gas mark 6).

Taking one ball at a time, place on a flour-dusted work surface, then gently press outward with your fingers. Leave the outer edge unpressed at this stage as you want to keep the air in so that it puffs up when baking. Continue to press outwards until it's about 20cm in diameter. Gently lift the dough and allow gravity to stretch it further, turning it in your hands until it's approximately 25cm in diameter. Transfer to a baking sheet lined with parchment paper and repeat.

Meanwhile, heat a large frying pan over a medium heat. Add the butter and tip in the leeks. Season with salt and pepper and sauté for 3–4 minutes, until beginning to caramelise. Stir in half of the chives.

Drain the artichokes and cut into quarters, reserving the oil in a small bowl. Brush the entire tops of the pizzas with the oil. Scatter over two-thirds of the fontina and mozzarella, leaving a 1cm border as a crust.

Arrange the artichokes and caramelised leeks on top of the pizzas and scatter the rest of the fontina and mozzarella on top. Bake for 10–12 minutes, until the crust is golden. Once cool, portions can be covered in cling film and kept in the fridge or frozen.

Slide the pizzas onto a chopping board and scatter over the remaining chives along with the basil, a few dressed salad leaves, the Pecorino and a light drizzle of the spiced honey. Cut into slices to serve.

15 MINS

 35 MINS

Roasted Tomatoes and Garlic with Goats' Cheese Serves 4

500g baby plum tomatoes

8 garlic cloves, peeled and squashed with a sharp knife

1 tsp tiny fresh thyme sprigs

1 tsp tiny fresh rosemary sprigs

2 tbsp olive or rapeseed oil

1 ciabatta loaf, sliced

2 x 150g logs of fresh goats' cheese, roughly chopped

150g natural yoghurt

finely grated rind of 1 lemon

1 tbsp chopped fresh flat-leaf parsley

sea salt and freshly ground black pepper

TO SERVE

black olives

roasted Spanish almonds (optional)

This is an amazing way to intensify the flavours and the resulting pile of soft, sticky tomatoes are spooned over soft goats' cheese so that it all melts into each other. I've served this with toasted ciabatta, but it could also be tossed into gnocchi or perhaps drizzled with a little pesto. Alternatively, serve with some good fresh pasta or a grain such as spelt or quinoa.

Preheat the oven to 180°C (350°F/gas mark 4).

Put the baby plum tomatoes in a baking dish. Scatter over the garlic, thyme and rosemary, season with salt and pepper, then drizzle over the oil. Roast, tossing once, for 20–25 minutes, until the tomatoes are blistered and beginning to burst.

Meanwhile, heat a griddle pan over a high heat until it's smoking hot. Toast the slices of ciabatta on both sides until nicely marked.

Mix the goats' cheese, yoghurt, lemon rind and four of the roasted garlic cloves in a bowl and season to taste. Tip onto a plate, then smear to the edge of the plate with the back of a spoon, making a well in the middle. Spoon the hot tomatoes into the well and scatter the parsley on top.

Serve family-style at the table with a basket of the toasted ciabatta and bowls of olives and almonds to serve, if liked.

15 MINS

 25 MINS

 LOADS OF VEG

 FREEZER FRIENDLY (NOODLES)

5 tbsp sunflower oil

2 aubergines, cut into 1cm cubes

320g dried egg noodles (6 nests)

4 garlic cloves, minced

½ tsp Chinese five-spice powder

2 tbsp miso paste

2 tbsp soy sauce

1 tbsp rice wine vinegar

1 tsp honey

1 tsp toasted sesame oil

4 eggs

4 spring onions, very thinly sliced

1–2 tbsp ChanChan Black Garlic and Peanut Rayu

freshly ground black pepper

Aubergine Black Garlic Noodles with Crispy Fried Eggs Serves 4

An Asian-style triple garlic sauce that makes the most mouth-watering noodles. This version takes them to the next level by using a black garlic peanut rayu made by Kwanghi Chan, a talented chef you might have seen on TV. Born in Hong Kong but raised in Buncrana, Co. Donegal, Kwanghi's fabulous ChanChan products have excellent distribution and can be found in the Sheridans sections of Dunnes Stores, Asian supermarkets and lots of specialist food stores.

Heat half of the oil in a large wok over a high heat. Stir-fry the aubergines in batches for 3–4 minutes, until softened and just starting to brown in places. When you're done, add all the aubergines back into the wok.

Meanwhile, cook the noodles in a pan of boiling water for 1 minute less than the packet instructions, then drain, reserving the water. Rinse the noodles in a colander in the sink to stop the cooking process.

Add two-thirds of the garlic to the aubergines, sprinkle over the five-spice and continue to cook over a low heat for a few minutes, until the garlic is golden and caramelised.

Put the miso paste in a tall container with the rest of the minced garlic and the soy sauce, rice wine vinegar, honey and sesame oil. Add 3 tablespoons of the reserved water from the noodles and blend to a silky-smooth sauce.

Heat the remaining sunflower oil in a large non-stick frying pan until it's smoking hot, then break in the eggs and cook for 1–2 minutes, until crispy around the edges, spooning the oil over the yolks to help them cook.

Add the noodles to the aubergines, then pour over the sauce. Cook for another 1–2 minutes, adding another splash of the water if the sauce is too thick.

Divide the noodles between bowls and add a crispy fried egg to each one. Season with pepper, sprinkle over the spring onions and drizzle with the black garlic peanut rayu to serve.

30 MINS

 1 HR

 LOADS OF VEG

❄ FREEZER FRIENDLY

1 large red pepper, cut into chunks

1 large red onion, cut into chunks

2 tbsp rapeseed oil

3 sweet potatoes, peeled and cut into slices 2cm thick

2 garlic cloves, minced

1 tsp chopped fresh rosemary

40g butter

1 bunch of spring onions, thinly sliced

150g baby spinach leaves

3 tbsp cream

2 eggs

1 x 250g carton of ricotta cheese

4 tbsp freshly grated Parmesan cheese, plus extra shavings

1 x 400g tin of chopped tomatoes

2 tsp red wine vinegar

1 tsp chilli flakes

6 sheets of filo pastry, thawed if frozen

sea salt and freshly ground black pepper

TO SERVE

rocket and pine nut salad

Crispy Greek-Style Filo Pie
Serves 4

This pie came about when there was nothing much in the fridge. The prep can be done while other elements are cooking.

Preheat the oven to 220°C (425°F/gas mark 7).

Put the pepper and onion on a baking sheet lined with parchment paper and drizzle over half of the oil. Toss to coat and season, then cook in the oven for 25 minutes, until tender.

Meanwhile, toss the sweet potatoes in the rest of the oil on a baking sheet lined with parchment paper. Season, then roast for about 15 minutes, until tender. Scatter over the garlic and rosemary for the last few minutes.

Heat a knob of the butter in a non-stick frying pan over a medium to high heat and quickly sauté the spring onions for 1 minute. Tip in the spinach, then season and sauté for another minute or so, until wilted. Pour in half of the cream and bubble down. Transfer to a bowl and snip with scissors into small pieces, then mix in the eggs, ricotta and Parmesan. Season to taste.

Tip the roasted pepper and onion into a bowl with the tomatoes, vinegar, chilli flakes and the rest of the cream. Season and blitz to a purée.

Melt the rest of the butter in a small pan. Unroll the filo pastry and cut each sheet in half again. Brush a little of the butter into a shallow baking dish. Use four pieces of the filo to drape all over the tin, brushing with butter. Cover with the sweet potato, then use the spinach and ricotta mixture to cover them completely. Spread with an even layer of the roasted pepper purée, then pull up the sides of the pastry. Use the rest of the filo to cover, gently scrunching it up, then brush with the rest of the butter. This can be covered with cling film and kept in the fridge or is perfect for freezing.

Reduce the oven temperature to 180°C (350°F/gas mark 4). Bake the pie for 25–30 minutes, until the pastry is crisp and golden brown. Cut into slices and serve on plates with the salad and Parmesan shavings.

CHAPTER 4 ALL-TIME FAVOURITES

30 MINS + 20 MINS RESTING

 2½ HRS

 FREEZER FRIENDLY

1 oven-ready whole Irish duck,
at room temperature (preferably
Thornhill – see the intro)

1 orange, cut into quarters

5g fresh thyme

1 tbsp rapeseed oil

FOR THE ROASTIES

1kg potatoes, peeled and cut into
large chunks

1 tbsp semolina

2 tsp onion granules

1½ tsp dried sage

FOR THE SAUCE

3 tbsp balsamic vinegar

3 tbsp orange blossom honey

2 tbsp tomato ketchup

1 tbsp soy and ginger sauce

1 tbsp light muscovado sugar

6 whole cloves

500ml fresh beef stock

sea salt and freshly ground black
pepper

TO SERVE

steamed purple sprouting broccoli

Thornhill Duck with Sage and Onion Roasties Serves 4–6

Thornhill is about a mile down the road and I've been using their duck for over 30 years. My good friends Ken and Sorcha Moffitt breed ducks that are a cross between a Pekin and Aylesbury, making them incredibly succulent. Ken is now supplying oven-ready ducks to selected supermarkets and butchers and they are worth tracking down.

Preheat the oven to 180°C (350°F/gas mark 4).

Keep the duck in the foil tray it comes in and remove all other packaging. Stuff the cavity with the orange and thyme, then smear it all over with the oil and season with pepper. Pour 100ml of water into the tray and roast for 1½ hours.

Meanwhile, cook the potatoes in a pan of boiling salted water until they are beginning to soften around the edges, then let them steam dry for a minute or so. Mix the semolina, onion granules and sage and season generously. Tip the potatoes into a roasting tin. Remove the duck from the oven and carefully drain about 3 tablespoons of the fat and juices from the tin, then pop the duck back in to finish cooking.

Brush the potatoes all over with the duck fat juices, then sprinkle over the semolina mixture, turning to coat. Roast for 1 hour, turning once, until crisp and golden brown.

To make the sauce, heat a sauté pan over a medium heat. Pour in the vinegar and bubble down, then whisk in the honey, ketchup, soy and ginger sauce, sugar, cloves and stock. Simmer until reduced by half, then season to taste and strain into a clean pan, ready to reheat.

The duck needs to cook for 2¼ hours in total or until it's golden brown and tender and the drumsticks feel nice and loose.

Transfer the duck to a warm platter to rest while you finish cooking the potatoes. Help this along by increasing the oven temperature to 200°C (400°F/gas mark 6).

Strain the sauce into a jug and pile the sage and onion roasties around the duck. Serve straight to the table family-style with the broccoli.

30 MINS + MARINATING

 2 HRS

 LOADS OF VEG

 FREEZER FRIENDLY

1 x 2kg whole chicken (preferably free-range or organic)

1 x 500ml can of beer

rapeseed oil, for drizzling

4–6 potatoes (each about 200g)

FOR THE MARINADE

100ml red wine vinegar

2 hot dried chillies

6 mild fresh red chillies

6 garlic cloves

1 tbsp smoked paprika

1 tsp dried thyme

1 tsp dried oregano

1 tsp light brown sugar

juice of 2 lemons

sea salt and freshly ground black pepper

TO SERVE

tomato and red onion salad with parsley

butter pats

lemon wedges

Piri-Piri Chicken with Jacket Potatoes Serves 4-6

Cooking chicken on a beer can is nothing new – they've been doing it for years in Australia and the US. The secret is that the beer keeps the inside of the chicken nice and moist. Of course, it can just be oven roasted in the normal way or spatchcocked and barbecued. If you don't like it too hot, adjust the number of chillies in the marinade.

To make the marinade, put the vinegar in a pan with the dried chillies and bring to the boil. Remove from the heat and cool, then pour into a NutriBullet or food processor. Add the fresh chillies, garlic, paprika, thyme, oregano, sugar and lemon juice. Blitz to a smooth paste.

Place the chicken in a shallow non-metallic dish and use a small knife to score all over with small cuts that are no more than 1cm deep. Pour over the marinade, then using your hands (a pair of plastic gloves is a good idea here because of the chillies), massage the chicken all over, inside and out. Cover with cling film and chill for at least 2 hours but overnight is best.

Preheat the oven to 180°C (350°F/gas mark 4). Remove the top shelf so that the upright chicken will fit.

Open the can of beer and pour about a quarter of it into a small, sturdy roasting tin. Give the marinated chicken another good smear in the marinade, then place it upright over the beer can and drizzle over the oil. Roast in the oven for 1 hour.

Put a criss-cross cut into the top of each potato and wrap it in tin foil. Pop the potatoes in around the chicken directly on the oven shelf. Cook for another 30–35 minutes, until a crust has formed on the outside of the chicken and the drumsticks move easily when gently tugged. Leave to rest for 20 minutes while the potatoes finish cooking, then cut into portions and carve the breasts into slices.

Arrange the chicken on a platter and pile the jacket potatoes alongside. Serve with a plate of tomato and red onion salad and separate dishes of butter and lemon wedges.

30 MINS + MARINATING

 25 MINS

 LOADS OF VEG

 FREEZER FRIENDLY

4 tbsp milk kefir or natural yoghurt

2 garlic cloves, chopped

2.5cm piece of fresh root ginger, chopped

2 mild fresh green chillies, roughly chopped

2 tbsp cream

1 tbsp rapeseed oil

5 green cardamoms, cracked for seeds only

1 tsp ground cumin

½ tsp grated nutmeg

25g mature Cheddar cheese, grated

4 tbsp melted butter

675g boneless, skinless chicken breasts or thighs, cut into 2cm pieces

FOR THE SABJI

1 tbsp rapeseed oil

1 onion, finely chopped

1 courgette, cut into 2cm cubes

1 large sweet potato, cut into 3cm cubes

50g frozen peas

2 tsp garam masala

1 tsp freshly grated root ginger

1 tbsp crushed roasted peanuts

sea salt and freshly ground black pepper

Chicken Tikka Skewers with Sweet Potato Sabji Serves 4–6

TO SERVE

boiled basmati rice

spiced mango chutney

fresh coriander sprigs

Authentic chicken tikka is traditionally cooked in a tandoor, or clay oven, but I think you can get some good results under the grill or a barbecue would also work well. The cheese is my secret ingredient that adds a pleasant creaminess to the dish. I've served it with a dry sweet potato curry that helps to ensure you get plenty of veg.

Place the kefir or yoghurt in a NutriBullet or small food processor with the garlic, ginger, chillies, cream, oil, cardamom seeds, cumin, nutmeg, Cheddar and half of the butter. Season generously and blitz to a smooth paste. Pour over the chicken and stir to coat. Marinate for at least 1 hour but overnight is even better.

Soak 8–12 wooden skewers in cold water for 15 minutes to prevent them from burning. Preheat the grill to high.

To make the sabji, heat a wok over a medium heat. Add the oil and stir-fry the onion, courgette, sweet potato and peas. Season to taste, sprinkle over the garam masala and continue to stir-fry for 3 minutes. Pour in 100ml of boiling water, then cover with a lid and simmer for 5 minutes. Remove the lid and simmer for another 5 minutes, until the vegetables are tender.

Meanwhile, thread the chicken onto the skewers and arrange them on the grill rack. Cook for 5 minutes, then turn over and brush with the rest of the melted butter. Cook for another 5 minutes, until the chicken is cooked through and lightly golden.

Stir the ginger into the vegetables and transfer to a serving bowl, then scatter the peanuts on top. Arrange the chicken tikka skewers on a platter and garnish with a few fresh coriander leaves. Serve family-style with a bowl of basmati rice and a small dish of the chutney.

30 MINS + CHILLING

 1½ HRS

 LOADS OF VEG

 FREEZER FRIENDLY

1 tbsp rapeseed oil

200g smoked bacon lardons

2 large leeks, cut into 2.5cm rounds

3 carrots, halved lengthways and cut into 2.5cm slices

2 celery sticks, finely chopped

2 bay leaves

2 fresh thyme sprigs

100ml white wine

50g butter

75g plain flour

600ml chicken stock

100ml cream

1 tbsp Dijon mustard

5g fresh tarragon leaves, chopped

1 whole rotisserie chicken (preferably free-range)

75g ready-to-eat prunes, finely chopped

1 x 320g pack of ready-rolled puff pastry

1 egg, beaten with a little milk

sea salt and freshly ground black pepper

Cock-a-Leekie Pie
Serves 4–6

This special pie takes notes from the hearty Scottish soup, which can be traced back to the eighteenth century. The sweet prunes and leeks balance the smoked bacon, enhancing the rich chicken and tarragon-infused sauce. The joy is using a rotisserie chicken and a sheet of pastry to create a standout family meal.

Heat the oil in a large frying pan over a medium to low heat. Sauté the lardons for about 5 minutes, until they have released their fat and begun to turn golden. Using a slotted spoon, transfer them to a large bowl. Add the leeks, carrots, celery, bay leaves and thyme to the pan, season generously and sauté for about 10 minutes, until the leeks are soft. Pour in the wine and allow to bubble for a few minutes, scraping the bottom of the pan with a wooden spoon. Tip the vegetables into the bowl with the lardons and discard the cooking herbs.

Return the pan to a medium heat and melt the butter. Add the flour and cook for 2–3 minutes, stirring. Add the stock a little at a time, stirring until smooth. Bring to the boil, stirring until thickened. Add the cream and mustard and allow to bubble down for a few minutes. Season to taste, then fold in the vegetables and lardons with the tarragon.

Peel the skin off the chicken and shred the meat into large chunks. Place in a 2.75-litre round pie dish or enamel roasting tin. Scatter the chicken over the bottom, followed by the prunes, then spoon over the sauce to cover completely. Use the puff pastry to cover the pie dish and crimp the edges against the dish, using a little of the beaten egg to make sure it sticks. Cut a small cross on top, then brush the top with the beaten egg too. The pie can be covered with cling film and kept in the fridge or frozen.

To cook, preheat the oven to 200°C (400°F/gas mark 6). Bake for 35–40 minutes, until bubbling and golden. Serve straight to the table.

20 MINS

 30 MINS

Cajun Chicken Melts
Makes 4

4 chicken fillets (preferably corn-fed)

1 tbsp rapeseed oil

2 heaped tsp Cajun spice

4 tbsp sweet chilli sauce

3 tbsp mayonnaise

4 small ciabatta rolls

150g extra-mature Cheddar cheese, grated

2 tsp ready-made pesto

200g mixed green salad leaves

FOR THE BALSAMIC DRESSING

3 tbsp extra virgin olive oil

1 tbsp balsamic vinegar

1 tsp honey

1 tsp Dijon mustard

sea salt and freshly ground black pepper

This is a firm favourite in the Maguire household. It's a great dish for a sudden influx of hungry people – so fast and easy to prepare. Everybody can help and you'll have it on the table in no time at all.

Preheat the oven to 180°C (350°F/gas mark 4).

Put the chicken in a baking dish and rub with the oil, then scatter over the Cajun spice and season with salt and pepper. Pour about 4 tablespoons of water into the dish around the chicken to ensure it stays lovely and moist. Roast for 18–20 minutes, until just cooked through and tender. Leave to cool, then cut into slices.

Mix half of the sweet chilli sauce in a small bowl with the mayonnaise and season to taste. Slice the ciabatta rolls in half and arrange on a baking sheet lined with parchment paper. Spread over the chilli mayonnaise and arrange the chicken slices on top in an overlapping layer. Cover with the Cheddar cheese and drizzle the rest of the chilli sauce on top in zigzag lines, then finish with the pesto in a similar fashion. Bake for 10–12 minutes, until the cheese is bubbling and lightly golden.

Meanwhile, to make the balsamic dressing, put the oil, vinegar, honey and mustard in a tall container with 2 tablespoons of water and blend until smooth, then season to taste. Put the salad into a bowl and use enough of the dressing to lightly coat the leaves.

To serve, cut each Cajun chicken melt in half again on the diagonal and arrange on plates with some of the dressed salad.

15 MINS

 45 MINS

 LOADS OF VEG

 FREEZER FRIENDLY

4 skin-on chicken fillets (ideally corn-fed or free-range)

½ tsp paprika

a knob of butter

FOR THE POTATOES

675g baby new potatoes

1 tbsp rapeseed oil

finely grated rind of 1 lemon

6 garlic cloves, unpeeled

1 tsp fresh thyme leaves

FOR THE SPINACH

250g baby spinach leaves

a knob of butter

1 onion, finely chopped

2 garlic cloves, crushed

2 tbsp plain flour

300ml milk

a pinch of ground nutmeg

25g mature Cheddar cheese, finely grated

FOR THE CARROTS

400g baby carrots

1 tbsp rapeseed oil

1 tsp honey

a squeeze of lemon juice

sea salt and freshly ground black pepper

Roast Chicken with Smashed Potatoes and Veg Serves 4

This is a fantastic alternative to a yummy roast chicken dinner delivered in under an hour. The creamed spinach is perfect instead of the more traditional gravy and the slightly caramelised roasted baby carrots cut through the richness perfectly.

Preheat the oven to 200°C (400°F/gas mark 6).

Put the potatoes in a large pan of water and bring to the boil, then reduce the heat and simmer for 10–15 minutes, until just tender – this will depend on their size. Drain.

Tip the potatoes into a large roasting tin and drizzle with the oil, then season and add the lemon rind, whole garlic and thyme. Toss the potatoes to coat, then use a potato masher to gently crack each potato, being careful not to break them up too much.

Place the chicken on top of the potatoes and rub over the paprika, then season and add a small knob of butter to each fillet. Roast for 25 minutes, until cooked through and tender.

Meanwhile, to make the creamed spinach, pour a kettle of boiling water over the spinach in a colander in the sink. Leave to cool.

Melt the butter in a pan over a medium heat. Add the onion and sauté for 4–5 minutes. Stir in the garlic and flour and cook for another minute. Gradually add the milk a little at a time, stirring continuously until you have a smooth sauce. Bring to a simmer and season to taste.

Squeeze any liquid out of the spinach, then roughly chop. Add to the sauce with the nutmeg and season to taste. Transfer to a small baking dish and scatter over the cheese.

Put the carrots in a small baking tin with the oil and season. Pop the carrots and spinach into the oven – they should slot in side by side. Bake for 15 minutes, until the spinach is bubbling and the carrots are roasted. Drizzle the honey and lemon juice over the carrots and toss until evenly coated.

Arrange the roast chicken on plates with the smashed potatoes, creamed spinach and baby carrots or serve family-style.

20 MINS

 30 MINS

 LOADS OF VEG

 FREEZER FRIENDLY

1 tbsp rapeseed oil

3 chicken fillets, cut into chunks

2 garlic cloves, crushed

1 onion, thinly sliced

2 red peppers, cut into chunks

1 x 400g tin of chopped tomatoes

4 tbsp light muscovado sugar

2 tbsp soy and ginger sauce

2 tbsp apple cider or balsamic vinegar

2 tbsp sweet chilli sauce

1 tbsp cornflour mixed with 1 tbsp water

1 small ripe pineapple, peeled, cored and cut into cubes

100g sugar snap peas, sliced

2 spring onions, finely sliced

2 tsp toasted sesame seeds

FOR THE RICE

200g basmati rice

a small knob of butter

Sweet and Sour Chicken
Serves 4

Don't call the takeaway – cook your own sweet and sour chicken using lots of veg and a fresh pineapple. Swap the chicken for pork or prawns if you prefer. Use this method to cook basmati rice and get perfect, fluffy results every time.

Heat the oil in a sauté pan over a medium heat and cook the chicken cubes for 3–4 minutes, until just starting to colour. Stir in the garlic and cook for 20 seconds, then tip in the onion and peppers and sauté for another minute or two.

Add the tomatoes along with the sugar, soy and ginger sauce, vinegar and sweet chilli sauce. Bring to a simmer, then cover with a lid and simmer for 5 minutes.

Meanwhile, rinse the rice in a sieve and put in a pan with a tight-fitting lid. Pour in 400ml of water, add a good pinch of salt and the butter and bring to the boil – this will take about 8 minutes. Whisk the rice in the pan to make sure it's well distributed. Put the lid on, turn the heat down as low as possible and simmer gently for 8 minutes, then whisk briefly again, remove the pan from the heat and cover with the lid, leaving it to steam until needed.

Stir the cornflour mixture into the sweet and sour chicken, then add the pineapple, sugar snap peas and spring onions. Cover again and simmer for 5 minutes, until nicely thickened. Season to taste. The sweet and sour chicken and the cooked rice can be covered with cling film and kept in the fridge or frozen.

To serve, spoon the basmati rice into bowls with the sweet and sour chicken and scatter over the sesame seeds.

Christmas Muffuletta Sandwich
Serves 4

1 round loaf of sourdough bread

3 tbsp mayonnaise

1 tsp Dijon mustard

1 tsp honey

2 tbsp red onion chutney

4 slices of Emmental cheese

150g thinly sliced cooked turkey

6 cooked pork sausages, halved lengthways (or 200g sausage stuffing)

3 slices of applewood smoked Cheddar

4 slices of cooked roast gammon or ham

3 tbsp cranberry sauce, plus extra to serve

25g baby spinach leaves

4 tbsp crispy onions

sea salt and freshly ground black pepper

TO SERVE

good-quality salt and vinegar crisps

A traditional muffuletta sandwich consists of a round loaf of bread split horizontally and filled with layers of delicious Italian ingredients. This version makes for the perfect festive sandwich but is just too good to have only once a year.

Slice a 3cm lid off the top of the loaf. Scoop out most of the bread from the loaf and the lid, leaving a 1cm layer (blitz these into breadcrumbs and use another time).

Mix the mayonnaise, mustard and honey together in a small bowl and season to taste.

Spread the red onion chutney all over the inside of the loaf, then add a layer of Emmental cheese followed by a layer of turkey. Spread half of the flavoured mayonnaise on top, then add a layer of the cooked sausages or the sausage stuffing. Add the applewood smoked Cheddar and a layer of roast gammon or ham. Add a good smear of the cranberry sauce and finish with the spinach. Scatter the crispy onions on top and smear the top with the rest of the flavoured mayonnaise.

Press the top down lightly, then tightly wrap the loaf in cling film. Now comes the most important part: you need to press it down and apply some weight. A small chopping board with a couple tins of beans is perfect. Leave it weighted down for at least 3 hours in the fridge but overnight is even better.

Cut into wedges to serve with some crisps and a small dish of cranberry sauce alongside.

20 MINS

 1 HR

 LOADS OF VEG

❄ FREEZER FRIENDLY

500g ham fillet (unsmoked)

a few black peppercorns

1 bay leaf

2 tbsp prepared English mustard

3 tbsp light muscovado sugar

FOR THE CAULIFLOWER CHEESE

1 large cauliflower

25g butter

25g plain flour

600ml milk

150g mature Cheddar cheese, grated

2 tbsp cream

a pinch of grated nutmeg

sea salt and freshly ground black pepper

Glazed Ham with Cauliflower Cheese Serves 4

A traditional cauliflower cheese but served with an excellent addition of a glazed ham. Adding a couple tablespoons of cream to the sauce really does change the flavour and makes it so much more luxurious.

Place the ham in a large pan with the peppercorns and bay leaf, then cover with cold water. Cover with a lid and bring to the boil, then reduce the heat and simmer gently for 30 minutes.

Cut the cauliflower into florets, reserving the small green leaves. Cook in a pan of boiling salted water for 3 minutes, then add the leaves and cook for another 2 minutes. Drain well and tip into a 2-litre baking dish.

Meanwhile, to make the sauce, melt the butter in a pan over a medium heat. Add the flour and cook, stirring, for 1 minute. Gradually stir in the milk, bring to a simmer and cook, stirring until thickened. Stir in 100g of the cheese with the cream and nutmeg. Season to taste.

Preheat the oven to 220°C (425°F/gas mark 7).

Carefully remove the ham from the pan and place in a roasting tin lined with parchment paper. Score the fat in a diamond pattern, then spread over the mustard and sprinkle the sugar on top. Cook in the oven for 20 minutes, until the glaze is bubbling and golden. Remove from the oven and leave to rest for at least 10 minutes.

Pour the sauce over the cauliflower and scatter over the rest of the cheese. Bake for 20 minutes, until the sauce is bubbling and the cauliflower is tender. The cauliflower cheese and the glazed ham can be covered with cling film and kept in the fridge or frozen.

Carve the ham into thin slices on a small chopping board and serve straight to the table family-style with the cauliflower cheese.

10 MINS + MARINATING

 30 MINS

 LOADS OF VEG

Seared Steak Tacos
Serves 4

juice of 1 lime, plus extra wedges to garnish

3 tbsp olive oil, plus a little extra for cooking

2 tsp ground cumin

2 tsp smoked paprika

4 garlic cloves, crushed

2 x 225g sirloin steaks (dry-aged if possible)

2 red onions, cut into wedges

1 red pepper, cut into 1cm slices

1 orange pepper, cut into 1cm slices

8–12 corn tortillas

1 romaine lettuce, shredded

2 ripe avocadoes, stoned, peeled and sliced

FOR THE CREMA AND SALSA

finely grated rind and juice of 1 lime

200ml soured cream

1 x 200g jar of pickled jalapeños, drained

20g fresh coriander, leaves stripped and stalks chopped

200g mixed red and yellow cherry tomatoes, diced

sea salt and freshly ground black pepper

Serve these steak tacos on a large board in the centre of the table with plenty of accompaniments and allow everyone to dig in. If you do make it in advance just make sure that you allow the steaks to come back up to room temperature before cooking.

Put the lime juice in a shallow non-metallic dish and add the oil, cumin, smoked paprika and garlic. Add the steaks and turn to coat, then add the onion wedges and peppers, tossing to take up the rest of the marinade. Cover with cling film and marinate for at least 20 minutes at room temperature or up to 24 hours in the fridge.

To make the crema, put half of both the lime rind and juice in a NutriBullet or mini blender. Add 2 tablespoons of the soured cream, a couple slices of jalapeño peppers and the coriander stalks. Blitz to a purée, then transfer to a bowl and stir in the rest of the soured cream and season to taste. Cover with cling film and chill for up to 24 hours in advance.

To make the salsa, finely chop a couple more jalapeño slices and mix with the tomatoes and the rest of the lime rind and juice. Season to taste. Cover with cling film and chill for up to 24 hours in advance. Tear in the coriander leaves just before serving.

Heat a griddle pan over a high heat and warm the tortillas until lightly marked on one side only, then wrap them in a clean tea towel to keep warm.

Brush the griddle pan with a little oil and cook the steaks for 2–3 minutes on each side or until cooked to your liking. Transfer to a plate and loosely cover with tin foil. Leave to rest while you cook the vegetables.

Toss the onions and peppers well in the remaining marinade, then chargrill in batches for 2–3 minutes on each side, piling them up on a serving platter or board as you go.

Add the bowls of crema, salsa and the rest of the jalapeños to the platter or board along with the lettuce and avocados. Thinly slice the steaks and garnish with the lime wedges and reserved coriander leaves. Unwrap the tortillas and serve everything family-style at the table.

15 MINS

 15 MINS

Smash Burgers
Makes 4

4 soft sourdough or brioche buns

2 tbsp chunky burger sauce

4 tsp mild American mustard

4 tsp tomato ketchup

400g beef mince (30% fat)

1 tbsp vegetable oil

4 slices of cheese

25g iceberg lettuce, finely shredded

2 gherkins, cut into slices

sea salt and freshly ground black pepper

TO SERVE

chips (optional)

These are a relatively new phenomena – think slightly charred, extra-juicy beef patty and gooey cheese in a pillowy soft bun. This is achieved by wrapping the whole thing up in foil for a few minutes before serving. If you're getting your mince from a butcher, ask for coarse ground, but the most important part to these burgers is getting mince with a higher fat content than you would normally go for – this is what gives them their unique flavour.

First dress the burger buns so that you can work quickly at the end. Smear the bottoms with the burger sauce, mustard and ketchup.

Heat a large non-stick frying pan over a high heat. Divide the mince into four meatballs. Add the oil to the pan, then add the meatballs. Put a piece of parchment paper on top, then smash them down as thinly as possible with the bottom of a heavy-based pan.

Remove the parchment paper, then season the burgers with salt and pepper. Cook for 3–4 minutes, then flip over, cover each one with a slice of the cheese and cook for another minute. Add a pile of lettuce and gherkins on top. Put one patty on each burger bun bottom, then press on the tops of the buns. Wrap each one in foil for a few minutes to let the steam do its magic.

Serve immediately on warm plates with some chips, if liked.

20 MINS + DOUGH THAWING

 40 MINS + 10 MINS COOLING

 FREEZER FRIENDLY

Salami Pizza Roll
Serves 4

1 x 500g packet of frozen sourdough dough balls (Golden Bake), thawed

a little plain flour, for dusting

100g Italian tomato sauce (from a carton or jar), plus extra for dipping

240g grated pizza cheese (mixture of mozzarella and Cheddar)

75g grilled mixed peppers from a jar, well drained

1 x 100g packet of Milano salami

40g pitted black olives, halved

1 x 210g mozzarella pearls, drained

1 tbsp fresh basil pesto (from a carton)

a small handful of fresh basil leaves

olive oil, for brushing

TO SERVE

mixed leaf salad

My kids love this novel way of making pizza. Feel free to vary the fillings depending on what you fancy and sometimes I put out an extra bowl of the pizza sauce for dipping.

To defrost the dough balls, thaw them according to the packet instructions – just remember to allow them to come back to room temperature before using.

Preheat the oven to 200°C (400°F/gas mark 6). Lightly dust your work surface with flour.

Take the thawed dough balls and knead them together to make one large ball, then roll out until you have a rectangle measuring about 30cm x 35cm.

Spread the tomato sauce over the dough, leaving a 2.5cm border around the edges. Scatter over the grated pizza cheese. Add a layer of the roasted peppers and salami. Scatter over the olives and mozzarella balls and drizzle with small dollops of the pesto, then tear the basil leaves on top.

Working from one long side, carefully roll up the pizza dough like a Swiss roll. Pinch the seam and the ends closed and transfer to a baking tray lined with parchment paper, seam side down. Brush with oil, then cut a few light slashes through the top layer of the dough. This can be covered with cling film and frozen.

Bake for 25–30 minutes, until cooked through and golden brown. Leave to cool for 10 minutes before cutting into slices and serving on plates with some salad and extra tomato sauce for dipping.

30 MINS

 30 MINS

Steak with Creamy Mushroom Sauce Serves 4

4 striploin steaks (see the intro)

2 tbsp rapeseed oil

3 fresh thyme sprigs

500g baby new potatoes

400g purple sprouting broccoli

20g butter, cut into cubes

FOR THE SAUCE

1 tbsp rapeseed oil

4 chestnut mushrooms, halved and thinly sliced

1 banana shallot, thinly sliced

3 garlic cloves, crushed

20g butter, cut into cubes

200ml cream

1 tbsp chopped fresh flat-leaf parsley

a squeeze of lemon juice

sea salt and freshly ground black pepper

The size of the steaks you get depends on your family and how hungry they are. However, as a rule, allow 150–200g for an adult and 100g for a child. I always try to buy Irish Angus steaks that have been matured for 28 days for the best flavour.

Twenty minutes before you want to cook, remove the steaks from the fridge, place them in a shallow dish, drizzle over the oil and thyme.

Steam the potatoes for 15–20 minutes, until cooked through and tender, then cut in half and pop into a bowl. Steam the broccoli for 2 minutes, then refresh under cold water and dry on kitchen paper. These vegetables can be made in advance and kept covered in the fridge.

Heat a large non-stick frying pan over a medium to high heat. Season one side of the steaks with salt and pepper. Drain off the oil from the steaks and add to the pan, swirling to heat it up. When the oil is almost smoking hot, add the steaks, seasoned side down, and tip in the thyme from the marinade. Cook for a minute or two, then add half the butter and swirl the pan so that it mixes with the oil. Cook the steaks for 2½ minutes, then turn over and cook for another 2½ minutes for medium rare, basting the steaks with the juices in the pan – cook them for a few minutes longer if you prefer your steak more well done. Transfer the steaks to a warm plate, cover loosely with tin foil and leave to rest for 10 minutes.

Tip the cooked baby potatoes into the pan that you cooked the steaks in and sauté for 8–10 minutes, until nicely golden.

Meanwhile, make the sauce. Heat a separate non-stick frying pan with the oil, then add the mushrooms and shallot. Season and sauté for 2–3 minutes, then add the garlic and butter and sauté for another minute. Pour in the cream and allow to bubble down and reduce for 2–3 minutes. Stir in the parsley and add lemon juice to taste.

In a separate pan, toss the broccoli in the rest of the butter to just warm through and season with a pinch of salt.

To serve, carve the steak into slices and arrange on plates. Spoon over the mushroom sauce and add the sautéed potatoes and broccoli.

30 MINS

 20 MINS

 LOADS OF VEG

Griddled Lamb with Artichoke and Butter Bean Salad Serves 4

1 x 290g jar of marinated artichokes in olive oil

4 x 150g lean lamb steaks

1 tsp dried oregano

a squeeze of lemon juice

100g semi sun-dried tomatoes in olive oil, drained and chopped

2 garlic cloves, crushed

½ tsp fresh thyme leaves

¼ tsp chilli flakes

100g black Kalamata olives, pitted

1 x 400g tin of butter beans, drained and rinsed

200g feta cheese, cut into large cubes

2 x 200g cartons of tzatziki

a handful of fresh mint leaves

2 Little Gem lettuces, cut into wedges

sea salt and freshly ground black pepper

This is just the kind of recipe I want to make when the sun is shining and I don't want to spend too much time in the kitchen. Of course, the lamb steaks would also cook brilliantly on the barbecue. You'll be transported to a Greek island in no time!

Drain 2 tablespoons of oil from the artichokes and put it in a shallow dish. Add the lamb, oregano and lemon juice. Season with salt and pepper and mix well to combine.

Heat a griddle pan over a high heat. Add the lamb steaks and cook for 2 minutes on each side, then transfer to a plate and leave to rest for 10 minutes, loosely covered with tin foil.

While the lamb is resting, drain the rest of oil from the artichokes and put it in a bowl. Cut the artichokes in half, then add to the griddle pan and chargrill for a minute or two on each side. Add back into the oil.

Add the semi sun-dried tomatoes to the bowl with the garlic, thyme, chilli flakes, olives and butter beans. Gently stir to combine, then add the feta and lightly mix again but not too much or you'll break up the cheese too much. Season with pepper.

Divide the tzatziki between the plates, spreading it out onto the side of each plate, then spoon over the artichoke and butter bean salad. Carve the lamb steaks into slices and arrange on top, then tear over the mint leaves. Add some Little Gem wedges or put them in a separate bowl, drizzling over any remaining dressing that is left over from the salad to serve.

20 MINS

 20 MINS

 LOADS OF VEG

 FREEZER FRIENDLY

400g lamb mince

2 garlic cloves, finely grated

2.5cm piece of fresh root ginger, finely grated

1 fresh red chilli, deseeded and finely chopped

1 lemongrass stick, very finely chopped

2 tbsp chopped fresh coriander, plus extra sprigs to serve

1 tbsp chopped fresh mint, plus extra leaves to serve

1 tbsp Thai fish sauce

FOR THE PICKLE

1 small red onion, thinly sliced

100ml rice wine vinegar

3 tbsp caster sugar

2 garlic cloves, minced

1 fresh red chilli, deseeded and finely chopped

finely grated rind and juice of 1 lime

2 tbsp fish sauce

½ cucumber, thinly sliced

50g radishes, thinly sliced

FOR THE SWEET CHILLI MAYO

4 tbsp mayonnaise

2 tsp sweet chilli sauce

sea salt and freshly ground black pepper

Thai-Style Lamb Burgers with Pickles Makes 4

TO SERVE

4 sesame seed burger buns

1 Little Gem lettuce, leaves separated

For a change, make these as meatballs and serve them in crisp lettuce leaves instead of burger buns.

Start by making the pickles. Put the red onion in a bowl with a pinch of salt and cover with boiling water. Set aside for a few minutes to soften.

Put the vinegar and sugar in a pan and bring to a simmer. Remove from the heat and stir in the garlic and chilli. Pour into a jug and stir in the lime rind and juice and fish sauce. Drain the red onion and put back in the bowl, then pour over half of the liquid. Put the cucumber and radishes in a bowl and pour over the rest of the liquid. Set aside for 10 minutes to allow the flavours to develop. Both these pickles will last covered with cling film for up to two weeks in the fridge.

Mix the mayonnaise and sweet chilli sauce in a bowl and season.

Heat a griddle pan over a high heat. Put the lamb in a bowl and add the garlic, ginger, chilli, lemongrass, coriander, mint and fish sauce. Season with plenty of pepper and mix well to combine, then divide the mixture into four portions and shape into patties. These burgers can be layered between pieces of parchment paper and frozen.

Add the lamb burgers to the hot griddle and cook for 5 minutes on each side, until cooked through and lightly charred. Transfer to a warm plate to rest, then lightly char the burger buns on the same pan.

To serve, add the lettuce to the bottom halves of the buns, then add some of the cucumber and radish pickle, draining it from the liquid. Top each one with a lamb burger, then add the red onion pickle and some coriander and mint. Finish with the sweet chilli mayo and burger bun tops.

20 MINS + THAWING

 50 MINS

 FREEZER FRIENDLY

300g sausage meat

400g pork mince

2 onions, finely chopped

100g semi sun-dried tomatoes, finely chopped

50g freshly grated Parmesan cheese

20g fresh flat-leaf parsley, leaves chopped

500g packet of frozen puff pastry, thawed

1 x 290g jar of grilled mixed peppers, drained

1 egg, beaten

1 tsp fennel or sesame seeds

sea salt and freshly ground black pepper

TO SERVE

crisp mixed salad

tomato relish

Neven's Sausage Plait
Serves 4-6

This sausage plait has all the flavours of my favourite sausage rolls. Here I have it as a main meal, but you could also serve it at room temperature or as part of a picnic. It can be cooked from frozen – just increase the cooking time by about 10 minutes.

Preheat the oven to 200°C (400°F/gas mark 6). Line a baking sheet with parchment paper.

Mix the sausage meat in a bowl with the pork mince, onions, sun-dried tomatoes, Parmesan and parsley. Season generously with salt and pepper.

Roll out the pastry in one piece measuring about 35cm x 40cm. Form the filling into a long flat log that will run the whole length of the pastry but only to cover the centre third of the pastry, leaving a 2cm gap at each end. Cover the sausage mixture with a layer of the peppers in an attractive pattern.

Use a small sharp knife to make 5cm diagonal strips in the pastry down either side of the sausage filling, spaced 1.5–2cm apart, then fold in alternately to create a plaited design and seal the ends. Brush with the beaten egg and sprinkle over the fennel seeds. This can be kept covered in the fridge or frozen.

Place the sausage plait on the lined baking sheet and bake for 40 minutes, until cooked through and golden brown. To test if it's ready, insert a metal skewer into the centre of the plait and hold it there for 3 seconds. Pull it out and tap it on the inside of your wrist – if it's too hot to hold there for more than 1 second, then it's cooked through.

Carve into slices on a chopping board and serve family-style with the salad and relish.

20 MINS

 1 HR

 LOADS OF VEG

❄ FREEZER FRIENDLY

100g plain flour

2 eggs

150ml milk

8 good-quality pork sausages

1 onion, thinly sliced

2 tbsp rapeseed oil

¼ tsp fresh thyme leaves

FOR THE GRAVY

1 tbsp rapeseed oil

1 onion, thinly sliced

2 tsp plain flour

2 tsp prepared English mustard

2 tsp Worcestershire sauce

300ml fresh beef stock

1 tbsp redcurrant jelly

FOR THE VEG

200g fine French beans

200g frozen peas

a knob of butter

sea salt and freshly ground black pepper

Toad in the Hole
Serves 4

Fluffy Yorkshire pudding batter studded with hearty pork sausages alongside a generous serving of rich onion gravy with plenty of veg on the side is a perfect midweek family meal. Make sure you buy good-quality sausages from the butcher or choose a premium range from the supermarket. Experiment with the flavour, such as spring onion and black pepper or chilli and cheese.

Preheat the oven to 220°C (425°F/gas mark 7).

First make the batter. Put the flour in a bowl and break in the eggs, then slowly mix in the milk. Beat until smooth.

Place the sausages in an ovenproof baking dish, scatter over the sliced onion and drizzle the oil on top. Roast for 15 minutes.

Remove the dish from the oven and pour the batter over and around the sausages, then return to the oven and cook for another 35 minutes, until the sausages are cooked through and the batter is golden on top. Scatter over the thyme leaves.

Meanwhile, make the gravy. Heat the oil or butter in a non-stick frying pan over a medium heat. Add the onion and sauté for 5 minutes, until golden. Sprinkle over the flour and cook, stirring until thickened. Stir in the mustard and Worcestershire, then gradually add the stock, stirring until smooth. Stir in the redcurrant jelly and simmer for 2–3 minutes, until thickened to a nice gravy consistency. Pour into a gravy jug when ready to serve.

Trim the French beans and place in a pan of boiling salted water with the peas. Simmer for 3–4 minutes, until tender, then drain and toss in the butter.

Serve the toad in the hole straight to the table family-style with the gravy and vegetables.

20 MINS

 25 MINS

 LOADS OF VEG

8–12 small soft flour tortillas

675g skinless cod fillet

2 tbsp fajita seasoning

rapeseed oil, for cooking

a little sweet chilli sauce

FOR THE SLAW

1 red onion, thinly sliced

1 small red cabbage, cored and very
finely shredded

juice of 1 lime

FOR THE PICKLED CHILLIES

100ml apple cider vinegar

50g caster sugar

4 fresh red chillies, deseeded and
sliced into rounds

FOR THE SAUCE

1 garlic clove, peeled

10g fresh coriander, plus extra
leaves to garnish

juice of 1 lime

1 tsp fajita seasoning

50g natural yoghurt

50g mayonnaise

sea salt and freshly ground black
pepper

Baja Fish Tacos
Serves 4

These Mexican-inspired fish tacos are served with purple slaw, pickled chillies and a generous drizzle of Baja sauce. Cod is the best fish as it flakes beautifully into lovely chunks but of course you could also use another firm white fish. Ask the fishmonger for a fillet that is even in thickness so that it cook evenly.

To make the slaw, put the red onion and cabbage in a bowl. Sprinkle over 1 teaspoon of salt, then add the lime juice and toss to combine. Leave for 20 minutes, stirring occasionally.

To make the sauce, put the garlic, coriander, lime juice, fajita seasoning, yoghurt and mayonnaise in a NutriBullet or mini food processor. Blitz until smooth and season to taste. Pour into a jug and add a splash of water if necessary to make it a consistency that can be drizzled. Cover with cling film and chill until needed.

To make the pickled chillies, heat the vinegar, sugar and 100ml of water in a small pan. Add the chillies and simmer for 2 minutes. Pour into a bowl and leave to cool. Cover with cling film and chill until needed.

Heat a griddle pan over a medium to high heat. Briefly cook the tortillas on one side, then wrap in foil to keep warm.

Dust the cod fillet in the fajita seasoning, shaking off any excess, then brush the griddle pan with oil. Cook the cod for 4–5 minutes on each side, until nicely charred and tender – you may need to do this in batches depending on the size of your pan.

Using a fish slice, transfer the cod to a plate and flake it apart with a fork. Place the cod flakes in a serving bowl and season with salt to taste. Garnish with the extra coriander leaves.

Serve straight to the table family-style with the tortillas, Baja sauce, purple slaw and pickled chillies. Have your favourite sweet chilli sauce to hand.

20 MINS

 30 MINS

 LOADS OF VEG

Salmon Parcels with Dill Yoghurt Serves 4

600g baby new potatoes, such as Charlotte or Jersey Royals

40g butter

4 spring onions, very thinly sliced

250g asparagus

200g purple sprouting or tenderstem broccoli

1 lemon

120ml vegetable stock

4 x 150g skinless salmon fillets

FOR THE DILL YOGHURT

150g Greek yoghurt

2 tbsp chopped fresh dill, plus extra sprigs to garnish

1 tbsp apple cider vinegar

1 tbsp wholegrain mustard

sea salt and freshly ground black pepper

A lovely light parcel of salmon with crisp green vegetables on a bed of a simple potato gratin, served with a light yoghurt dressing. These can be made in advance and chilled for up to 24 hours.

Preheat the oven to 200°C (400°F/gas mark 6).

Cut the potatoes into thin slices (about 3mm) and cook in a pan of boiling salted water for 6–8 minutes, until tender. Drain and return to the pan with the butter and the spring onions. Season to taste, then toss gently to coat.

Bring a large pan of salted water to the boil. Cut the asparagus and broccoli in half on the diagonal, cutting any thick broccoli stalks in half again lengthways. Add to the pan and blanch for 1–2 minutes, until just tender, then use a tongs to transfer to a bowl of iced water. Once cooled, drain well and dry on kitchen paper.

Pare the rind from the lemon into curls, then cut away four thin slices and cut the rest into wedges. Set aside until needed.

Cut four large squares of parchment paper and place them on your worktop. Divide the potato mixture between them, slightly scrunching up the sides, and spoon over 2 tablespoons of stock. Add the salmon fillets and season to taste. Nestle around the asparagus and broccoli and put a thin slice of lemon on top of each fillet.

Bring the sides of each parchment parcel together, folding and crimping the edges to seal, making sure there is still room for the air to circulate during cooking. Place two parcels on each baking tray. Bake the salmon parcels for 15 minutes, until puffed up.

Whisk the yoghurt in a bowl with the dill, vinegar and mustard. Season to taste and loosen with a splash of water if necessary to achieve a drizzling consistency.

To serve, transfer the parcels to plates and carefully open them up, as steam will be released. Scatter over the lemon rind and a few dill sprigs, then drizzle over the dill yoghurt. Serve the lemon wedges on the side.

20 MINS

 20 MINS

 LOADS OF VEG

Hot Smoked Salmon Salad with Baby Spinach and Potatoes
Serves 4

4 eggs

500g baby new potatoes

100g baby spinach leaves

1 shallot, finely chopped

3 tbsp olive oil

1 tsp apple cider vinegar

1 x 200g vac-packet of baby beetroot, halved or quartered

2 tbsp spiced nuts and seeds (such as Good4U)

4 hot smoked salmon fillets (about 300g)

1 x 50g packet of pea shoots

FOR THE DRESSING

120g soured cream

juice of ½ lemon

3 tbsp snipped fresh chives

1 tsp Dijon mustard

sea salt and freshly ground black pepper

This can be thrown together in minutes to make a fresh, vibrant salad that looks incredibly stylish. The combination of flavours is a match made in heaven, but you could use smoked salmon or trout if you prefer.

Place the eggs in a pan of boiling water and simmer for 7 minutes. Remove with a slotted spoon and cool down under cold running water, then peel off the shells and cut each one in half. Set aside until needed.

While the eggs are cooking, make the dressing. Place the soured cream in a bowl with the lemon juice, chives and mustard. Season to taste.

Meanwhile, place the potatoes in a large pan of boiling salted water and cook for 10–15 minutes, until tender when pierced with a sharp knife. Drain the potatoes, then cut into slices and add to the spinach with the shallot. Drizzle over the oil and vinegar and season to taste.

Spoon the baby spinach and potato salad onto plates and scatter over the beetroot and spiced nuts. Scatter over the flaked salmon, then drizzle with the dressing. Add the soft-boiled eggs and a good grinding of black pepper, then scatter over the pea shoots to serve.

20 MINS

 20 MINS

 LOADS OF VEG

 FREEZER FRIENDLY

1 tbsp rapeseed oil

a knob of butter

1 small onion, finely chopped

1 small leek, finely chopped

1 carrot, diced

1 potato, diced

225g fresh mussels, cleaned

150ml dry white wine

1 tbsp plain flour

500ml chicken stock

150ml cream

100g skinless salmon fillet, cut into cubes

100g natural smoked pollock fillet, cut into cubes

100g skinless whiting fillet, cut into cubes

100g raw peeled prawns

1 tbsp chopped fresh dill, plus extra to garnish

sea salt and freshly ground black pepper

TO SERVE

brown wheaten bread and butter

Hearty Seafood Chowder
Serves 4

This is a recipe that my mother loved to make and that I recently got to recreate while filming for a TV series in the beautiful seaside village of Howth. It relies on a variety of fish, so you'll need to take a trip to the fishmonger or you could use 400g of a seafood chowder mix. If you're in Dublin, Howth is hard to beat as there is a whole line of shops there so that you can compare prices!

Heat the oil in a sauté pan over a medium heat. Add the butter and once it stops sizzling, stir in the onion, leek, carrot and potato. Tip in the mussels and pour in the wine. Cover with a lid and simmer for 2–3 minutes, until the mussels have opened, discarding any that do not.

Using a tongs, remove the mussels and set them aside in a bowl. Sprinkle in the flour, stirring to combine, and cook for another minute, stirring continuously. Gradually pour in the stock, then pour in the cream. Cover again and simmer for 6–8 minutes, until the vegetables are tender. Stir in the fish and prawns and simmer gently for 2–3 minutes, until just cooked through.

Take the mussel meat out of the shells and return to the chowder, allowing it to just warm through. Season to taste and add the dill. This can be kept covered in the fridge or frozen.

Ladle the chowder into bowls and garnish with the dill sprigs. Serve with a separate basket of brown wheaten bread and a dish of butter.

25 MINS

 20 MINS

Lemon Sole Tempura with Cucumber Salad and Chips
Serves 4

sunflower oil, for deep-frying

900g potatoes (such as Rooster), peeled and cut into skinny chips

600g lemon sole fillets, skinned and cut into strips

FOR THE BATTER

50g plain flour

50g cornflour

175ml iced sparkling water

2 ice cubes

FOR THE CUCUMBER SALAD

1 large cucumber, peeled and thinly sliced

2 large gherkins, thinly sliced

3 tbsp rapeseed oil

3 tbsp white wine vinegar

2 tbsp chopped fresh dill, plus extra sprigs to garnish

sea salt and freshly ground black pepper

TO SERVE

mayonnaise spiked with lime rind and juice

lemon wedges

malt vinegar

This tempura batter is lovely and crisp but it needs to be made and used instantly. Don't worry about lumps, as they will actually improve the texture of the batter.

Preheat the oven to 150°C (300°F/gas mark 2).

First make the salad to allow the flavours to develop. Place the cucumber slices in a bowl with the gherkins, oil, vinegar and dill. Season with salt and pepper and set aside until needed.

Heat the oil in a deep-fat fryer or a deep-sided pan, making sure it's only half full, to 160°C (325°F).

Put the chips in a bowl of cold water. Drain and dry them as much as possible in a clean tea towel before placing them into the fry basket (you may need to do this in batches depending on the size of your basket) and lowering them into the hot oil. Fry for 4 minutes, until cooked through but not coloured. Drain on kitchen paper and set aside.

Increase the temperature of the oil to 190°C (375°F).

To make the batter, mix the flour and cornflour in a bowl, then whisk in the sparkling water and ice cubes. Season with salt. Dip the lemon sole into the batter, then quickly place in the hot oil and fry for 4–5 minutes, until crisp and golden brown (again, you will have to do this in batches). Drain on kitchen paper and keep warm in the oven.

Tip the blanched chips back into the fry basket and carefully lower into the hot oil. Cook for 1–2 minutes, until crisp and golden brown. Drain on kitchen paper.

To serve, divide the cucumber salad and the chips between small bowls and add to plates with a pile of the lemon sole tempura. Garnish with the dill and add a dollop of the lime mayonnaise and lemon wedges for squeezing over. Put a bottle of malt vinegar on the table.

20 MINS

 55 MINS

 LOADS OF VEG

1.2 litres vegetable stock

½ tsp saffron strands

1 tbsp rapeseed oil

a knob of butter

1 onion, finely chopped

350g risotto rice

150ml dry white wine

50g freshly grated Parmesan cheese, plus extra to garnish

FOR THE VEGETABLES

175g frozen broad beans

1 tbsp rapeseed oil

a knob of butter

2 small leeks, thinly sliced

2 garlic cloves, thinly sliced

4 tbsp dry white wine

1 bunch of fine asparagus, trimmed and cut into 2.5cm pieces

100g frozen peas

2 tbsp chopped fresh herbs (such as flat-leaf parsley, chives and/or chervil)

juice of ½ lemon

sea salt and freshly ground black pepper

Saffron Risotto with Green Vegetable Ragout Serves 4

This looks stunning and is incredibly easy to make. The saffron adds just the right touch of flavour and a dazzling colour without being overpowering. I've picked it up on my travels and have enjoyed many seasonal variations over the years.

Bring the stock to a gentle simmer in a pan. Heat a separate sauté pan over a medium to high heat. Add the saffron and heat, shaking the pan, for a minute, until the threads are dry, brittle and fragrant.

Add the oil and butter to the saffron, then tip in the onion and season generously. Sauté for 5 minutes, until softened but not coloured. Stir the rice into the onion and saffron mixture and cook for 1 minute, stirring, until the grains are well coated in oil and almost transparent. Pour in the wine and allow to bubble down for 1 minute, stirring.

Add a ladleful of the simmering stock and cook until it has been completely absorbed, stirring regularly. Continue to add the stock a ladleful at a time, making sure that each time you add the stock the previous amount has already been absorbed.

Blanch the broad beans in a small pan of boiling water, then drain and refresh under cold running water and pinch off the outer shells.

After 10 minutes, make the vegetable ragout. Heat a large non-stick frying pan over a medium heat. Add the oil and butter, then tip in the leeks and garlic. Season with salt and sauté for 4–5 minutes, until tender. Pour in the wine and allow to bubble down.

Add the asparagus and a splash of the stock from the risotto and simmer for a minute or two, until bright green and crisp tender. Add the broad beans and peas and cook for another 2 minutes. Remove from the heat and stir in the herbs and lemon juice. Season to taste.

After 25 minutes the rice should be cooked (al dente). Remove the pan from the heat, stir in the Parmesan and season to taste.

To serve, divide the risotto between plates and make a well in the centre, then spoon in the vegetable ragout and scatter over the Parmesan.

20 MINS

 25 MINS

 LOADS OF VEG

2 sweet potatoes, cut into 2.5cm cubes

½ tsp chilli flakes

½ tsp ground cumin

½ tsp ground cinnamon

4 tbsp olive oil

100g quinoa

1 tsp balsamic vinegar

juice of 1 lime

a handful of fresh coriander leaves

1 tub of salad cress

1 bunch of spring onions, thinly sliced

40g mixed sprouts

½ cucumber, diced

1 ripe avocado, peeled, stoned and cut into cubes

1 crisp round lettuce, trimmed and shredded

2 tbsp chilli nuts and seeds (such as Good4U)

100g pomegranate seeds

50g feta cheese

sea salt and freshly ground black pepper

Superfood Salad
Serves 4

This salad is packed full of delicious veggies and high-fibre quinoa. I like to top it with pomegranate seeds for a great burst of flavour. It's the kind of thing I make all the time as it's just so full of goodness but super satisfying at the same time.

Preheat the oven to 200°C (400°F/gas mark 6).

Put the sweet potatoes in a roasting tin with the chilli flakes, cumin and cinnamon. Drizzle with 1 tablespoon of oil and toss until evenly combined. Spread into an even layer and roast for 15 minutes, until tender and just starting to caramelise. Remove from the oven and leave to cool a little.

Meanwhile, cook the quinoa in boiling salted water for 15 minutes or according to the packet instructions. Drain and rinse well under cold running water.

Put the remaining oil in a bowl with the balsamic vinegar and lime juice. Stir in the quinoa, then tear in the coriander leaves and snip in the cress. Add the spring onions, mixed sprouts, cucumber, avocado and lettuce, stirring to combine. Fold in the roasted sweet potatoes and season with salt and pepper.

To serve, tip out onto a serving bowl. Scatter over the chilli nuts and seeds followed by the pomegranate seeds, then crumble the feta cheese on top.

20 MINS + CHILLING

35 MINS

FREEZER FRIENDLY

Goats' Cheese and Sticky Fig Relish Puffs Serves 4

2 x 320g packets of puff pastry, thawed if frozen

350g fresh goats' cheese, cut into 2cm slices

4 heaped tbsp sticky fig relish (see the intro)

1 egg

2 tsp sesame seeds

FOR THE SALAD

50g pecan nuts

1 tbsp Highbank Orchard apple syrup or honey

a knob of butter

1 chicory

1 x 100g bag of watercress, rocket and spinach salad

100g vac-packed baby beetroot, cut into quarters

2 tbsp extra virgin olive oil

2 tsp balsamic vinegar

sea salt and freshly ground black pepper

We are lucky to have so many excellent goats' cheese producers in Ireland – here I'm using a fresh goats' cheese like St Tola, which has no rind. I just adore this combination, so I've played around with the ingredients and come up with this recipe. It uses my sticky fig relish that is now available under the Simply Better range in Dunnes Stores.

Unroll one of the puff pastry sheets and cut it into quarters. Divide the goats' cheese slices between them, leaving a 2.5cm border around the edges, then add a heaped tablespoon of the sticky fig relish to each one. Crack the egg into a small bowl and whisk with a pinch of salt, then brush around the edges.

Unroll the second puff pastry sheet and cut it into quarters. Place a rectangle of puff pastry on top of the filling and carefully seal and crimp around the edges using a spoon. Score some lines on the top of each one and brush with the rest of the egg wash. Scatter over the sesame seeds and transfer to a baking sheet lined with parchment paper. Chill for 20 minutes to rest or this can be kept in the fridge or frozen.

Preheat the oven to 200°C (400°F/gas mark 6).

Bake the goats' cheese puffs for 20–25 minutes, until the pastry is cooked and looks puffed up and golden.

Cook the pecan nuts in a small baking tin alongside the goats' cheese puffs for 3–4 minutes, until toasted.

Heat a non-stick frying pan over a medium heat. Add the toasted pecan nuts, then drizzle over the apple syrup or honey and add the butter. Cook for a minute or two, until glazed and sticky. Tip out onto a piece of parchment paper and leave to cool.

Trim down the chicory and break into individual leaves, then gently toss in a bowl with the salad. Arrange on plates with the beetroot and drizzle over the oil and vinegar. Scatter over the caramelised pecan nuts and add a goats' cheese and sticky fig relish puff to serve.

Index